M000308413

SITTIN' ON DYNO-MIGHT! HOW TO MANAGE

YOU

for Success

A PROFESSIONAL GUIDE FOR MAXIMIZING YOUR
IMPACT BY UNLEASHING THE POWER OF

—— YOU ——

ANTOINE LANE

Sittin' on Dyno-might! how to manage YOU for success
Copyright ©2013 Antoine Lane
All rights reserved.
ISBN: 0615800300
ISBN 13: 9780615800301

Author's note: Events described in this book happened as remembered. Names have been changed to respect privacy and anonymity.

Library of Congress Cataloging-in-publication Data
Lane, Antoine p.cm.includes notes includes bibliographyLeadership II. Business practices—leadership III. Business—ethics

HF 5387 L66 2013658.11 La

DEDICATION

This book is dedicated to my very beautiful and supportive wife Stephanie a.k.a. "Carrie",

my parents Velma & Jesse

my sons Aaron and Bryce and the rest of my family Brian and Tina,

and especially to the new relationships that will be forged between author and reader.

Rochelle,
Positive. Infectious. Energy!
That is Rochelle!
Enjoy
A

ACKNOWLEDGEMENTS

There aren't enough acknowledgements that can be given to your parents when you consider their sacrifices, guidance and love. So allow me to fully acknowledge their efforts, especially my Mom. You did an amazing job, Mom! I hope you are proud. From the bottom of my heart, Thank YOU.

To Dr. Moody, the person most responsible for shaping my perspectives and showing me the path toward becoming a Kingdom man and a giver of talent, I say Thank YOU, Sir.

To Mindy Reed, my editor, who took a personal and professional interest in this project, I say Thank YOU.

And to all the people who have taught me, trained me, encouraged me or took a chance on me, I say Thank YOU – Joe S., Jayne P., Janice B., Tim E., Brad B., Trell B., John-John M., Kenny K., Shane L., Darrion H., Yong L., Theo C., Tom S., Mark L., Willz, Terry G., J.D.L., Celeste T., Michelle R., James J., Dr. Springer, Dr. Balanoff, Dr. Dietz, Dr. Garcia, Dr. Ibeneche-Nnewihe, Dr. Ferguson, Dr. Anderson, Barbara W., Jeff A., Allen M., Tim E., Ron L., Wayne D., Rich F., Dave D., Max J., Don F., Fred F., Mike M., and Art A.

CONTENTS

THE SERENGETI BIRTHDAY

The Serengeti Plains of Africa are a vast, wide-open region of flatland, home to predator and prey. As a pregnant gazelle searches for a suitable delivery location, she is short on options and without protection or privacy. So she does something very interesting. After lying down to give birth, the mother gets on her feet immediately, and with afterbirth still clinging from the youngling, she uses her nose to nudge the infant to its feet. Why? Because the mother knows that there are predators roaming nearby, and there's *life* for the youngling if she can just get the newborn to its feet. She knows that the babe is born with the gift of speed, agility and endurance—capable of out maneuvering nearly every predator on the plain. So she bumps and she pushes, and she pokes, urging the youngling to stand up. The babe tries to stand, then falls, but the mother is persistent. And after several failed attempts, the baby gazelle is on its feet. Stumbling to maintain its balance, the babe recognizes its mother and starts moving towards her. Amazingly, the babe begins to walk, still stumbling, but walking nevertheless. Within minutes the babe is modeling its mother, running right along side of her to safer ground.

What a birthday! Can you imagine how the baby must have felt being born into this strange, new world of competition for existence? We could assume that what the babe really wanted was to be coddled, allowed to suckle in the comfort of the mother's warm embrace while making sense of it's surroundings. Maybe the mother experienced similar emotions, but she knew all too well the challenges that lay before her offspring. So she temporarily set aside her desire to comfort her newborn, and assumed her responsibility to help unlock the babe's potential. She rendered out its unique gifts and unleashed this little dynamo to perform on the great stage of life.

In moments of stress and strife, faced by challenges and controversy, many of us yearn to be coddled and comforted. Such a response provides only temporary relief. However, we benefit from having our innate qualities recognized and succeed when we are shown the tools needed to use those qualities to maximum benefit.

That's what *Sittin' on Dyno-Might!* is all about. Like the mother gazelle, I have been blessed with the ability to help others recognize their unique qualities and unlock their potential. The following chapters provide the reader with the tools needed to unleash the power resident within them to perform on life's biggest stages.

Life is a timed exercise that requires strength, endurance and stamina. So get up....get on your feet...and let's get running!

CHAPTER 1

REFLECT

Inspired by a desire to exist with a heightened state of renewal that provides motive for rehabilitation of the soul.

Taking a look into the proverbial mirror can sometimes be a scary proposition. We're encouraged to confront what we find, rather than embrace what we see. If you truly desire to be renewed, and wish to improve your humanity, one of the most difficult tasks of self-reflection is to try and see something when you have no idea what to look for.

In 1991 I embarked on a journey to become a police officer. Public service is a noble occupation and I have always been motivated by a strong sense of fairness. But after nearly five years, six tries and three different departments, I was yet to be hired. For those of you who are unfamiliar, the hiring process is lengthy and emotionally taxing. If you're not hired on the first try, the constant rejection can leave you feeling demoralized. After about the fourth year, I was beginning to wonder if I'd ever get the opportunity to *serve and protect.* But I remained focused and continued to pursue my dream.

I finally made it to the last phase of the hiring process and was sitting in front of the hiring review board. It had been nearly three hours, and I had fielded what seemed like a thousand questions, when the high-ranking commander who was chairing the board simply stared at me. In fact all the board members were staring at me. I kept telling myself, "Hang tough...don't fall to pieces now!" Then after a long, awkward silence that seemed like an eternity, the commander looked at me over the glasses that were sitting on the bridge of his nose and said, "I'm gonna give you a chance kid. And you better not let me down." Almost saluting in my chair, I quickly replied, "I won't Sir. You have my word."

Six months later, I graduated from the police academy and was assigned to a beat. I was a fast learner. I quickly garnered the respect of my peers, as well as the bad guys who lived in my district. I had a lot to prove (so I thought). I became known as a "dope hound"—a street cop who specializes in street level narcotics arrests. Being a dope hound was a high profile style of policing that lent itself to a healthy dose of foot pursuits, vehicle pursuits and physical altercations just like you see on television. Talk about fun! I was a kid in a candy store with a pocket full of quarters.

As I look back and reflect on some of my early years, I recall one particular incident that should have been a life altering moment for me. But because I didn't have the self-awareness to recognize the true value of reflection, I went on several more years without "... *a desire to exist with a heightened sense of renewal.*"

It was the mid 1990s when crack cocaine still gripped most inner cities. Coupled with high gang recruitment, at risk youth found it simply too irresistible to pass up some fast cash in the dope game. On one particular night I noticed a youngster near a well-known street corner for narcotics sales. I passed by him several times earlier in the night while heading to other high priority calls. Finally, the dispatch radio was quiet enough for me to inquire about this individual's plans for the evening. By now he had probably become complacent based on the earlier drive-bys, so I made it appear as if I was headed to yet another high-priority call when suddenly I stopped my car and made contact with him. I radioed to the dispatch -

Me: Charlie 705.

Dispatch: Charlie 705 go ahead.

Me: Show me out on a subject near Harmon Street.

Dispatch: 10-4.

He was alarmed by my approach, turned and immediately began walking away. We both made small talk as we strolled along. He kept looking nervously over his shoulder as he spoke. Both of us were fully aware of what was about to happen; yet we continued to engage in this very strained dialogue between us. I maintained a constant vigil on his hands to eliminate the possibility of him producing a weapon, and to identify any contraband. Then I saw it. With the skill of a magician he deftly ridded his person of a small quantity of crack cocaine using a slight of hand street technique called the "cup and pitch." As I stopped briefly to retrieve the dope from the ground, he decided the jig was up and the chase was on!

His initial escape attempt was witnessed by a small group of citizens that was, how shall I say, less than enthusiastic about the nobility of law enforcement. One of them said to the laughter of his companions, "You're never gonna catch him." To which I immediately shouted back as I ran by, "Watch me!"

Now with most foot pursuits, if you're able to simply keep the runner in your line of sight, they'll start to fade and eventually run out of gas. But this young man had fuel to burn so I summoned for help on my handie talkie. The muffled sounds of wind and movement urgently came across the air as I transmitted my location to the dispatcher:

Me: Charlie 705 – foot pursuit near the 1200 Block of Harmon Street! Subject is now running westbound on 13th Street!

Dispatch: I need a unit to start for Charlie 705, in foot pursuit Of a subject near the 1200 block of Harmon...now westbound near 13th.

Charlie 704: Charlie 704, myself and Charlie 707 are not far off.

Dispatch: 10-4. Charlie 704 and 707 enroute.

Me: Now running northbound on Collins Street.

Dispatch: Now running northbound on Collins.

Charlie 704: Roger that.

Me: Suspect is wearing a white t-shirt, blue shorts, black tennis shoes—now hopping a fence in the 2600 block.

Dispatch: Charlie 705 I copied a white t-shirt, black shorts... repeat your last...

Charlie 707: He said black tennis shoes. I have them in sight... they're cutting into the backyard of...standby.

Me: (Muffled transmission that was inaudible)

Dispatch: 705 10-9 your last transmission. Repeat, say again repeat! Anybody copy that?

Charlie 707: They're fighting! Back of 2603! 2603 Collins street! Out on them!

As more cops responded to the scene, the night erupted to the sound of sirens and screeching tires, and the whole neighborhood was beginning to light up like a Christmas tree. The fleeing subject had scrambled to get away, darting back and forth across the street. I caught a break when he was about to jump a fence and we both heard the unraveling of a thick chain and the deafening bark from a dog that could be none other than Cujo. The suspect had second thoughts and climbed down, giving me the opportunity to close the gap between us. He finally faded and I was able to catch up to him, although it was a considerable distance from our original starting point. He initially resisted arrest, but had expended too much energy during his escape. So after employing a couple of police techniques I was able to finally apprehend the subject. Exhausted and barely able to speak myself, I quoted his rights between deep, gasping breaths, "You...have the right...to remain.......silent."

Several officers responded to our location as we emerged from in between the houses. Charlie 707 offered to give us a ride back to my patrol cruiser, but I declined. I had other motives in mind. As I started walking with the subject back to my police unit, a second officer offered to assist me with a ride, but I rudely waived him off too. Although I was muddy, sweating profusely and dog-tired, I continued to march this perpetrator toward my police unit, even jeering at the subject saying, "What happened captain? What's the matter partner? You tired? Thought you were goin' get away, huh?"

As we rounded the corner leading to my car, the naysayers were still in their front yard. I proudly marched my "collar" past them but didn't say a word. I just looked at them, and the look on my face said it all. At first, they didn't say anything either. For just a moment, it seemed as if we were frozen in time. We were all reflecting on what had just happened, contemplating where we stood on the matter: Me, the perp, the naysayers, even the cops who were slowly driving in a line behind us as if we were in a parade. Suddenly the silence broke in the small crowd of onlookers with a mixed chorus of admiration of my capture, and admonishment for how I did it.

In hindsight, this was the first opportunity that I received feedback about the incident, and for a moment, it gave me pause to think. How must the suspect have felt being dishonored in such a fashion? What were the thoughts of the people in the crowd? What did my colleagues think of me at that moment? Right or wrong? Ethical or unethical? Fair and just, or ugly and unreasonable? What do you think?

JUSTIFICATION

I could probably justify my actions by asking you to consider the perspective of a 25 year-old rookie police officer wishing to change the world. Would you be willing to make allowances for this young, prideful professional doing his part to contribute to society? After all, he was challenged and he met that challenge with courage, resolve and a successful outcome. You may agree with my actions or even make some concessions about how I behaved, but justification is the enemy of authentic reflection. Justification will never provide you *motive for the rehabilitation of the soul*. What justification can do, however, is create a pattern of behavior that habitually absolves wrongdoing, mitigates culpability, and drastically impedes personal, professional and spiritual growth.

After securing the prisoner in the back of my patrol car, we headed to jail. There was silence. No dispatch chatter on the radio, and neither of us said a word. As a light drizzle began to fall from the night sky, we were stopped at a particularly long red light when something happened. I felt something. The feeling was faint and distant and only lasted for a brief moment, but I recall it feeling uneasy. I began having flashbacks in my mind over and over again about what had just taken place between the suspect and I. After having made the decision to grandstand my capture of him, making a spectacle of the arrest, something inside me begged to be reconciled. Unknowingly, I came to the proverbial fork in the road—to the left: justification for my actions—and to the right: authentic reflection of my actions and embracing how the entire experience could mature me as a human being. I ignored this slight tug on my conscious, largely because it was unfamiliar and...to be perfectly honest with you...because it was a bit scary.

Unbeknownst to me at the time of his arrest, this would not be the last time that I chased and arrested C.J. Swinford. As fate would have it, C.J. and I were inextricably bound, and our paths would continually cross over the next fifteen years regarding a wide variety of infractions of the law. No matter the situation or circumstance, we would always end up discussing what took place the first night we met. The quiet tranquil ride we experienced that first night was a thing of the past. C.J. was a verbal riot every ride after that. Every time C.J. expressed his dissatisfaction of the treatment he received that night, I readily offered him a reason for my actions. To me it was simple: you're a drug dealer; I'm a cop. Cops arrest drug dealers. That's what cops do. Illicit drugs deprive people of a fruitful existence, devastate families and ruin communities. It only takes one time to be at the scene of a teenage accidental drug overdose for you to carry extreme prejudice against drug dealers. Drug dealers are the scum of the earth! I continued to put as many drug dealers in jail as I came across and was content with the fearful reputation I acquired amongst their kind. *Justification.*

In retrospect had I genuinely contemplated my interactions with C.J. as a whole, maybe I could have encompassed a bigger picture. First, the assumption that I made about the naysayers being in direct opposition to any enforcement of the law that would, in my mind, only serve to give them a higher quality of life. Come to think of it, I don't recall that I ever formally introduced myself to them. My field-training officer told me that the people in the neighborhood weren't particularly fond of police officers, so I believed him instead of finding out for myself. It's rather ignorant to presuppose that an entire neighborhood would feel the same way about anything.

Secondly, by rejecting the help of my comrades-in-arms I inadvertently created a barrier between us. Law enforcement is about teamwork. You're taught in the academy that lone super heroes "get dead." But remember, I had a chip on my shoulder because it took me so long to get on the police force. Maybe I was grandstanding my capture of C.J. in front of the cops in an effort to distinguish my talent from my peers. I recklessly assumed that they probably made it on the police department on their first try and looked down on a guy who took six attempts to make it. No matter the reasoning it hindered my development.

Thirdly, and most importantly, I was oblivious to the fact that people could change—even drug dealers.

After years of paying my dues on the street, I was eventually promoted to the rank of Detective and assigned to police headquarters. One day, I saw a couple of boys about eight or nine years old giving one of our child service workers a hard time. I've seen children come in to the main headquarters before, either needing transportation to a relative's home because their parent or guardian was arrested, or some other childcare issue, so this scene wasn't unusual. After listening to several unheeded warnings from the social worker to the boys regarding their behavior, I decided that maybe I could offer a stern warning to the young lads.

Having grown older and bit wiser over the years, I decided against my traditional approach of towering over the children in my uniform and formally addressing them. Instead I opted to kneel down and speak softly to them. Though I was in a shirt and tie, their eyes zeroed in on my gun and badge, but I could tell they appreciated this kind of approach. I seized the moment and quickly established some amicable dialogue. One of the boys just stared at me, almost in awe. He was contrite about his behavior and tried to answer my questions respectfully, but he seemed bewildered. We agreed that they would behave, so I returned to my desk feeling as if I made a positive impression.

Twenty minutes later, the child service worker came to my desk and thanked me for my assistance. She stated that the grandmother of one of the boys was there to pick them up and they wanted to say goodbye to me. Excited about the opportunity, I hurried back to the workers' station. I could tell that it was the starry-eyed boy who wanted to speak with me. As I approached, he asked in earnest, "Will you come to my school?"

Without a second's delay I responded, "Will you promise to behave?"

He smiled real wide and nodded his head 'yes' in an exaggerated fashion.

The adults laughed as I formally introduced myself. I said, "Hello, I'm Detective Lane."

"I'm Chester," he returned.

Later that same week, I was at Chester's school having lunch with him. Over the next several months I served as a mentor for Chester working very closely with his teachers in an effort to maximize his potential. As was the case with most of the children who attended Chester's school, he came from a broken home. His academic capability was self-evident, but his behavior was erratic and unpredictable. However, since I began meeting with Chester, his grades were more consistent, his inappropriate behavior was virtually non-existent and his doctors even lowered the dosage of medication he was taking. Unbelievable!

One day I invited Chester on a church field trip. To go, we needed to get consent from his parent or guardian. As I helped him fill out the waiver, it occurred to me that I didn't know Chester's last name. As he slowly wrote his name across the form, I was flabbergasted. He wrote Swinford. Immediately I looked up at him and said, "What's your father's name?"

He said, "Chester Swinford. And I'm Chester Jerome Swinford, Jr."

My jaw nearly hit the picnic table. Chester's dad is C.J. Swinford! I became flustered, started quickly collecting the forms and picking up our lunch while repeatedly apologizing—telling Chester that I could no longer mentor him. He did not respond well to put it nicely. I regretfully informed the school of the conflict of interest and asked to be reassigned to another child. The school's mentoring administrators agreed and I was paired with a child from another school.

The very next morning I received a call from Chester's school. As my cell phone continued to vibrate, I stared at the number prepared to stand my ground on the issue. To my surprise, the school administrator told me that C.J. Swinford himself was at the front office demanding that I continue to mentor Chester! I could hear C.J. in the background with that all too familiar C.J. tone and style—a street mixture of gibberish and profundity.

Puzzled, I pulled the phone away from my ear and stared at it for just a moment, and for reasons still unknown to me to this day, I decided to meet with C.J. and his son at the school the following Monday. With my cop instincts on high alert, I arrived early and was given a letter that C.J. had written to the mentor administrators. C.J. took full responsibility for his criminal history. He stated that his misguided past had hindered him as a father and he felt that I could serve as a positive role model in his son's life.

C.J. included a story in the letter about our relationship, but it wasn't the story about the first night we met. Unlike me, C.J. had reflected and matured from that fateful night. His story was about a more recent interaction between us where I didn't do anything special at all. He said I just talked to him. No official police commands. No law enforcement actions. No lecture or speech. I just talked to him. It was clear to me now that C.J. experienced authentic reflection. He reflected on our situation with a desire to be a better man, and he fearlessly embraced his "Self."

I however, remained stuck in the introductory mode of our relationship; resigned to justifying my actions. I can look back now and see that I had a chance to embrace my "Self" too. But justifications blinded me from *choosing* to do so.

"*you* & YOU"

Self is the real *"you"*—the raw bones, the alone staring in the mirror when no one else is around *"you"*. Without a desire to embrace the private *you, you* cannot improve the public "YOU." "YOU" is the combination of Self and the persona that we all work so devilishly hard to project in public.

This is a very critical concept for understanding this book, "*you* & YOU". They are one and the same, but have very different roles. With regard to the private *you*, no one has the right to make any demands of *you*. But when it comes to the public YOU, the world has the authority to order your conduct, and demand a particular manner of behavior from YOU, if YOU want to be successful. The focus of this book will be about **YOU**.

DYNAMO ALERT!

*There will be Dynamo Alerts throughout this book warning YOU about remaining the same, or challenging YOU to change. Here's the first Dynamo Alert for **YOU**—if you do not embrace Self, **you** cannot manage **YOU**. It's a daunting task, and not much fun, so we rarely do it. But it is imperative we take an honest look at ourselves, make a genuine assessment of our motivations, perspectives and actions, and embrace our true YOU.*

No one knows *you* better than *you*. We sometimes say that someone else knows us better than we know ourselves, but that isn't entirely true. When people say someone else knows them better, it is usually because they do not have the desire to confront the parts of themselves that are too painful, too embarrassing, or too humbling. The people who truly love us choose to accept all of our shortcomings, so we feel that they know us better than we know ourselves. But all they've really done is chosen to do something that we won't – choose to embrace all of YOU.

You must be willing to embrace all of YOU: the good and the not so good, the saint and the sinner, the average worker and the consummate professional. By accepting all of the genuine *you—you* are then able to modify the behaviors that keep *you* from being the very best YOU–YOU can be.

YOU are a complex creature: unique, yet the same as anyone else. YOU demand to be acknowledged, YOU covet companionship, and YOU desire to be affirmed. I invite *you* to take this opportunity to reveal YOU, and learn more about the best way YOU perform. The camaraderie of humanity is healthiest when *you* know more about YOU and the way YOU operate. Knowing more about the way YOU perform will enable YOU to live a "life in contention"— always contending for a chance to win. A life in contention must be done ethically, against our self-serving modes, long-winded justifications and poor excuses for our actions. And to help YOU do that, I'd like to introduce YOU to the **Dynamo Pak**.

DYNAMO PAK: "THE TOOLKIT"

The Dynamo Pak is an ethical toolkit that will assist YOU with how to practically apply the concepts and ideas annotated in each chapter. The goal of the Dynamo Pak is to enhance your professional development by creating a rapid learning cycle where YOU **Reflect**, and compare your life experiences with the principles of the Dynamo Pak. The Dynamo Pak will help to increase your capacity to perform at a high level by providing YOU with a starting point and guidelines for some of the challenges and obstacles that YOU will encounter in your given profession.

Now it would be impossible to cover every aspect of your professional life, so I have concentrated the focus of this book on some of the more common barriers that hinder performance and prohibit growth. But first, I'd like to offer YOU another tool for your journey—**S.H.O.E.S.**

S.H.O.E.S.

Dr. Charles A. Moody, Jr., creator of *"The 90 Minute Workout for Leaders*[1]*,"* teaches that in order to enhance the understanding of change, *you* must become cognizant of issues that either contribute to or impede your journey to successful leadership. Dr. Moody developed the acronym S.H.O.E.S. that stands for:

- **S**ociological factors
- **H**istory
- **O**pportunities or Oppositions
- **E**xpectations
- **S**piritual influences that sway the thoughts of the leader

Our upbringing, social circles, and history help to shape our perspectives. These aspects are very instrumental in helping us make determinations as to whether something is an opportunity for us, or if it is in opposition to our expectations. This occurs in every setting that we're placed in. Being more aware of these very powerful forces can greatly enhance your efforts to change. This is the first of many reminders but always remember everywhere *you* go, YOU are walking in your S.H.O.E.S.

CHAPTER 2

ETHICS

Obedience to a truth that immerses us in a fellowship of humanity and allows faith in a greater good to be the baton that we pass on.

Did you know that your attention might be the most expensive commodity on the planet? The top ten corporate giants in America spent an estimated $25 billion dollars on advertisement and marketing in 2011 alone.[2] That's billon with a "B." In fact, one company alone spent an astonishing four billion dollars on marketing. It is almost impossible to fathom the amount of money spent just to get our attention. The truth is that the CEOs of these corporations understand there is a direct correlation between your attention and their bottom line. It's the science of marketing strategy and competition.

People participate in these two social sciences daily, most of the time unknowingly. When you, the consumer shop for goods and services, you strategize your purchase. Regardless of the item or service, whether you are shopping for clothes, groceries, cars, homes, college tuition, stocks, property, or retirement plans, you levy the risks and rewards of that purchase against other competitive options. As a result, marketing strategy and competition become a way of life.

Marketing is not just an external phenomenon that is thrust upon us. Each of us are aggressive marketers when it comes to our own self-image. We are no different really, than the corporate giants we judged as opportunists a paragraph ago. Like them, we expend an enormous amount of resources towards marketing our self-image, sometimes at the expense of others. We believe that somehow looking "*better*" than them has a direct correlation on the success of our careers. We carefully craft the message that we want to broadcast, and then we spend an outrageous amount of energy orchestrating the desired outcome of our interactions with people.

Is this ethical behavior? Why do we do it? What motivates us to engage in such conduct? The answer is ego. We're motivated by a very strong natural inclination to enhance our self worth, while simultaneously protecting our image. This is why ethics is so important. Ethics provides mediation between our psychological survival instincts and our competitive participation in the marketplace. So is there anything wrong with devising a marketing strategy that makes your work product more attractive than your co-workers? Absolutely not. Unless it's done unethically. Is there anything wrong with pre-empting the competition for a more advantageous position? Absolutely not. Unless it's done unethically.

And is there anything wrong with using all of our *"Might!"* to compete for a high level promotion? Absolutely not. Just as long as it is done ethically.

After many years as a police officer, I went back to school to finish my undergraduate degree. Additionally, I obtained a Certified Public Manager's (CPM) license, and earned a Master's Degree in Training and Professional Development, with heavy academic emphasis in Human Performance Technology. This led to a parallel career as a corporate trainer. One of the major topics I've taught on has been ethics. When it comes to managing YOU for success, ethics has to be what centers *you* and guides your moral compass. When presented with an ethical dilemma, YOU cannot be motivated by selfish gain. Nor can YOU judge people based on your individual criteria of what is corrupt or immoral. Just as justification is the enemy of authentic reflection, the wrong motives can be the cancer of ethics.

CASE IN POINT:

Rod works for a car repossession company. He's a physically imposing man who is relatively quiet and always seems to have a smile on his face. He's highly intelligent, knows his job well and is consistently one of the top performers at his shop. But like nearly every other industry these days, the economy had taken its toll. Rod, who once averaged nearly ten repos a week, found himself lucky if he repoed a few cars a month. For Rod, no cars meant no paycheck.

Though he searched earnestly, Rod could not locate a repo and faced yet another week without a paycheck. He was already several months behind on his rent. Without a repo soon, Rod and his four sons would be out on the street.

Heading to the shop after yet another disappointing day, Rod spotted what he thought was a repo. It was an older model mini-van that had a spare tire attached to the rear bumper. An SUV pays double, so Rod was aware of the outstanding mini-van, but had been unable to locate it for several months. Excited about the find, Rod quickly checked his ledger, located the paperwork and then called back to the office to verify the status of the vehicle. The dispatcher Jane confirmed that the vehicle was outstanding. As was his routine, Rod re-checked the vehicle's identification numbers and license plates to ensure that he had the right car and then he backed his tow truck into the driveway to tow it away. "A find like this means a big paycheck for sure", Rod thought to himself.

Suddenly, a woman emerged from the residence screaming frantically with a thick foreign accent, "What are chu doin'? What are chu doin'?"

Rod calmly showed the woman the paperwork regarding the repossession orders, and asked, "Are you Tina Har—"

But she cut him off—"Yes, yes. What are chu doin'? HELP! HELP! So-body hel-me?"

Though he was embarrassed, Rod desperately tried to offer Tina an explanation, but it was useless. Tina refused to look at the paperwork and continued screaming for help. As if she were hugging the car, she rested her head on the hood of the car saying dejectedly, "Chu no unner stand. Chu no unner stand..."

Tina's neighbor, Will, heard her calls for help and confronted Rod. Rod attempted to explain to the neighbor the purpose of the tow, but with Tina screaming so loudly and Rod's tow truck running, it was difficult for them to communicate. The scene was chaotic as other neighbors started coming outside and peering from their apartment windows.

About that time, two small children appeared in the doorway of Tina's apartment. When she saw them, she quickly calmed herself and rushed over to comfort them.

Finally collecting herself, Tina wiped her tears turned to Rod and said as best as she could in broken English, "If chu take car... can child sea and bag-pack come witt-me? School tomorrow, yes?"

Rod paused for a moment. He wanted nothing more than to just leave, but he was hesitant. The mini-van was already loaded on the bed of his tow truck. All he had to do was drive away and he would make enough money to tie him over for the next couple of months.

As Tina pleaded for Rod to reconsider, Will chimed in, "Think about the kids, bro. What about them?" Rod felt the weight of a thousand eyes watching him. Suddenly, Rod's cell phone rang; he looked at the phone and saw it was Jane from the office. She was calling about his status since he hadn't checked in since the commotion began. Rod assured Jane that everything was fine and that he'd be at the shop shortly with the tow. As he ended the call with Jane, the smile returned to the big guy's face as he began lowering the bed of his tow truck to assist the mother.

Will formally introduced himself to Rod, and in very short order, they were laughing about the current state of affairs of their favorite pro football teams and their hopes for a trip to the Superbowl. Then, without warning, Tina placed the children inside the towed vehicle. Rod was momentarily dazed by her actions as he watched Tina secure herself and her children inside the mini-van. When Rod asked what she was doing, Tina placed her smartphone against the car window. To Rod's amazement, Tina had already bookmarked the webpage from the traffic code law that prohibited the tow of a vehicle with people still inside it.

Will who was also stunned, immediately began reprimanding Tina, but Rod was all too familiar with the law. And besides, it was against company policy to tow an occupied vehicle.

Tina said in a commanding voice from inside the car, "Lemme down, now! I will call police. I will sue...for safety oh the childs."

Will, disgusted by Tina's actions, encouraged Rod to call the police. But Rod knew this was a civil matter and the police had no bearing. He finished unhooking the vehicle and disheartened, he drove away.

After Rod left, Tina started the van and began backing out of the driveway. She saw Will standing at the curb, obviously troubled with this drastic turn of events. She looked up at Will, rolled down her window and said, "Don't judge me. I did what I had to do..."

MOTIVES

Many of us would deem Tina as being unethical, citing that she manipulated Rod by playing the role of a victim, when all the while she had corrupt motives and a premeditated plan in mind

from the beginning. Some might even say that she was resource-
ful, motivated by the welfare of her children. That's the tricky
thing about motives; we view the actions of others through our
personal definition on what is ethical or unethical. That is why it
is imperative that we submit to a higher standard of values that
drastically reduce our own biases and prejudices so that we are
not tricked by the emotions of our heart and hampered by our
S.H.O.E.S. (see Chapter 1).

Whether corrupt or pure, motives can be a slippery slope
when it comes to an ethical dilemma. We have to beat down our
survival instincts at times to allow our altruistic values to surface,
and monitor our subconscious desire to judge.

DYNAMO ALERT!

*The fellowship of humanity is healthiest when we
can strive toward a platform of understanding that is
less about motive and more about incentive, less about
judgment and more about understanding.*

For instance, your judgment of the characters in this story could
change in an instant. What if I told you that Tina was in an abusive
relationship for years and finally mustered up the courage to leave
her manipulative husband because she didn't want her children to
grow up thinking that it was okay to be abused? That she worked
as a waitress at a local diner and simply didn't make enough money
to cover the expense of rent, daycare costs and the car note? That
she refused to get on welfare and walked to work for months before

she bought the car? That she suffers from recurring nightmares of returning to the hellish lifestyle of a battered wife? Living far away from her native homeland, Tina was just trying to survive. Would that change your judgment of her? How so?

What if I told you that Will had a romantic interest in Tina, but didn't view the woman and her children as a package deal? That he only wanted a physical relationship with her from time to time? That his motives for inquiring about Rod weren't altruistic, but self-serving? He just wanted to know if Rod and Tina were romantically involved, yet he stood in disgust as he judged Tina. Would that change your judgment of him? How so?

And what about Rod? He was just trying to be a nice guy and was sent home empty-handed and may be out on the street. What if you discovered that Tina's husband befriended Rod, and told Rod where Tina was staying? That Rod was aware of the husband's abusive past, but needed the money for the repo? Would that change your judgment of him? How so?

Judging less and understanding more offers a chance at empathy. Somehow, when we seek inclusion vs. isolation, and have incentive to experience a vicarious existence vs. judging one another's actions from our own perspective, we are more apt to communicate trust in each other. And when we commit to trusting in a standard that is for the betterment of the whole, there's an opportunity to render success for anyone who acknowledges that standard. This is the intent of ethics.

ETHICS

Garnering people's attention about YOU by way of a marketing strategy isn't the secret for success as corporate America supposes. In fact, there's no secret for success at all, just a choice. An intentional choice that YOU make daily to exist within the confines of a behavioral system that's ethical, communal and not self-serving. One where the state of mind that suggests a total indoctrination in self-marketing for self-gain at all costs is not a pre-requisite for success.

Are you listening ENRON? Too late for them.

Are you listening Wall Street? Too late for them, too.

Are *you* listening YOU?

DYANAMO PAK: "HOW TO OVERCOME THE ETHICAL DILEMMA"

How to overcome the ethical dilemma? This is the age-old question that has somehow become the linchpin for teaching ethics. Though very similar, there are typically two schools of thought regarding *teaching* ethics. The first is to teach the theory of ethics didactically—through lecture with the intent to impart a moral lesson.[3] The second method is through the use of real life scenarios that require or compel people to make a decision, and learn from the process of their decision, thereby raising their ethical awareness. I espouse the latter.

We've already taken a look at our main characters from the story, Rod, Tina and Will, now let's focus on Jane. Jane is one of those inherently sweet people who would do anything to help you. Because Rod struggled to make ends meet, Jane volunteered to babysit his boys, even watching them as they played around the shop, waiting for their dad to get off work. Though she and Rod were not involved in an intimate relationship, Jane had grown close to the boys, even taking them to school some days. Consequently, Jane knew that Rod was about to be evicted and she couldn't bear the thought of those boys being homeless. Rod confided in her his fears of being homeless and dreaded the day that he would have to tell his boys. Rod practically begged Jane to help him find a repo. Jane hoped and prayed that Rod would get a repo and she did everything she knew how to do to help, but they were unsuccessful.

Jane however, had a secret. She knew Billy, Tina's abusive husband. Billy came to her six months prior lamenting about Tina taking the van and leaving him yet again. Billy knew the alias Tina was using to hide from him, and he wanted Jane to use her work computer to locate Tina, citing his desires to see his children. Knowing full well that it was against company policy, Jane refused and hadn't spoken to Billy since. "Besides," she reasoned, "they were going to do what Billy and Tina always did...get back together."

Jane struggled with this information about Tina's alias for a while, but finally justified in her mind that she had to do something to help Rod. She reasoned with herself saying, "Are YOU going to sit back and let those children go homeless? How could YOU look them in the face knowing that there was something that YOU could have done to help?"

So Jane made a decision. She used her work computer to search for Tina under the alias that Billy provided and found her. Jane then contacted Billy and arranged an introduction with Rod. The next day, Rod found the repo. Just like Tina, Jane did what she thought she *had* to do – help Rod or let those children go homeless. What would YOU do?

That's the clinical definition of an ethical dilemma: a moral conflict where obedience or commitment to one, results in a transgression against another. So how do YOU overcome such predicaments? There's no simple answer. The complexities of life prevent the invention of a "How To" manual for ethical decision-making. However, the starting point for YOU has to be adhering to an ethical standard that does not include personal biases and prejudices that prevent a holistic benefit to anyone who willingly conforms to that standard.

Because of the dynamics of human interactions there isn't a perfect plan on how to handle the realities of life, but here's a model that I'd like to offer that would help insulate YOU from some of the common pitfalls people face when attempting to overcome an ethical dilemma. It's called the **5 E's of Ethics: Embrace, Empathize, Evaluate, Endure and Expire.**

EMBRACE

When the circus of life leaves an elephant in the room, do not pretend it doesn't exist. YOU cannot embrace a solution until YOU can embrace the problem. This is not to suggest becoming confrontational on the job regarding any matter that bothers YOU, but be prepared to welcome an opportunity to rectify a problem.

The key is to embrace, not to confront. There's a difference between "confronting" a problem and "embracing" an issue. To confront is to meet with hostility. To embrace is to avail yourself to receive. YOU embrace the issue in the name of ethics. Animosity can threaten the balance of the workplace environment. Like the proverbial snowball, the longer YOU let it roll on, the bigger it will become. One of the ways that I've found beneficial for embracing workplace issues is to be mindful of **timing, technique and tension.**

Timing is about feel. There are more "Don'ts" than "Dos."

- Don't approach an individual at a time when they are emotionally compromised.
- Don't try to embrace a situation that is emotionally charged.
- Don't create an atmosphere where the person or persons feel trapped or ambushed.
- Don't schedule a conversation first thing in the morning, or last thing before the end of the day. I know this may be contradictory to what YOU have seen on the job, but from a performance standpoint, YOU don't want the dialogue of the conversation weighing on the person's mind all day if it's done first thing in the morning. And YOU don't want to wait until the end of the day because it is typically better for the person that YOU are dealing with to have a chance to return to some kind of workplace normalcy and finish the day on a high note. Just before lunch is a great target time. It allots a cooling

off period, a chance for everyone to get refueled and the opportunity for all parties involved to *Reflect*.

Technique is about having the right ingredients.

- First, privacy is essential. It is human nature to become protective when threatened and nothing is more threatening than to feel affronted by co-workers or supervisors in an open forum.

- Second, is delivery. Do not employ a machine gun listing of everything that the person has done over the last year and a half that has personally peeved YOU and your co-workers. People are more apt to receive when YOU have the right environment and tone, and just a single issue to target.

- Third, is attitude. Having the right tone is about having the right attitude. An attitude that is more related to *embrace* and less connected to *confront* will greatly enhance the proper tone.

- Fourth, have a mature, objective third party assist YOU. Someone who is ethical, fair and wise enough to understand the value of principles. Also keep in mind, YOU need to demonstrate as much a desire to resolve the issue as YOU exhibit in relaying the issue. In other words, use the same passion for developing solutions as YOU used in conveying the problem.

Tension is about effectively conveying to the person the company's commitment to operate under an ethical standard. YOU, as well as everyone in the group, must be held accountable for their behavior and method of communication. For instance, someone in your group tells a dirty joke over lunch. YOU may not have had a problem with the joke, but someone else was offended and later decided to *embrace* the transgression by meeting with the 'joke-teller.' They ask YOU to be the third party based on your ethical behavior and maturity. In your mind YOU can't figure out how the person could have possibly been offended by that joke. But this isn't about YOU. It's about protecting the sanctity of the ethics of the group. If the ethical standard of the group stipulates that anyone who is offended will embrace their issue with the offender, then YOU should adhere to your commitment to the ethical standard. So if someone is offended, they should select the right **time**, employ the proper **technique** and share with the offender their feelings. Getting everyone to conform to the ethical standard is the **tension**. It serves as the enforcement action [per se] in this instance, not the person who was offended. It is essential that YOU have a full comprehension of this definition of **tension**.

EMPATHIZE

Nothing livens up the dull atmosphere of the office like SCANDAL. Understand this, scandal is an intoxicant. It draws people together at work to gossip who otherwise wouldn't have two words to say to one another. Avoid the feeding frenzy, avoid the blame game, and avoid passing judgment. Instead, be a grace granter and empathize with those who are involved in an issue. The 'Repo' story clearly demonstrates the dangers of judgment.

Empathy does a couple of things.

- First, empathy helps to retrace the events leading up to the moment that everyone else is judging. The results of the scandal are often so sensationalized by the news, or over exaggerated by the office rumor mill, that it's difficult to view the truth of the incident in totality.
- Secondly, empathy mitigates the natural tendency that YOU have to impose your personal biases, perspectives and prejudices. YOU can't forget that you're always wearing your S.H.O.E.S.

EVALUATE

In private, and I must repeat, in private, give yourself a chance to judge all the people involved in the scandal or dilemma. This is in direct contradiction to what was just stated under Empathy, I know, but trust me—once YOU have empathized with the situation, go ahead judge them. Criticize them, pick a side, assess blame, run it through your personal filter, and come to a determination of the "How" and the "Why's", the "Rights" and the "Wrongs." Put on your judge's robe, climb high above your bench, detail for the jury and all those in attendance the many layers of recklessness, negligence and guilt on behalf of the defendants, and then grab your gavel and sentence them!

Now that those evildoers have been punished for their transgressions, do YOU a big favor and take a second look at the situation. YOU will be amazed at how clearly YOU see things objectively. YOU will also experience how therapeutic the use of this technique is for re-calibrating your own moral compass. During the Evaluate step, YOU might discover some perspectives YOU once had, have changed.

ENDURE

Of the 5 E's of Ethics, Endure may be the most significant for overcoming the ethical dilemma. Endure is where YOU must exercise patience. Not only is your patience required, but YOU also need to exhibit something I call, "Poker-face Professionalism." Those who are not directly involved in the ethical dilemma will be either *constructive* or *destructive*. Individuals who embrace the situation, grant grace, empathize and privately self-evaluate will help to rebuild the damage caused by the dilemma. Those who are confrontational, judgmental and have low self-awareness will contribute to tearing down the situation further. So when YOU come in contact with deconstructionists, display "Poker-face Professionalism." Do not concede to their over exaggeration of third-hand information; their misquote of news reports; or their seemingly innocent inquiry about "what happened?" What these people fail to realize is their integrity is at stake. People who can empathize; privately evaluate their position; remain non-accusatory; and refuse to contribute to the muck and mire of office drama, while maintaining a professional outlook, will grow as a leader in ways unimaginable to the deconstructionist.

EXPIRE

When the ethical dilemma has finally passed and those directly involved have been made accountable, LET IT GO! Do not provide CPR to a dead issue. Too often, past situations will be brought back to life and the drama re-lived, time and time again— long after it has been resolved for no worthwhile purpose. This has a devastating effect on young blood and fresh faces. Sharing the messy details of a past ethical dilemma with new personnel, without any relative teaching points, is irresponsible. LET IT GO!

5 E'S OF ETHICS:

EMBRACE. EMPATHIZE. EVALUATE. ENDURE. EXPIRE

- Welcome the opportunity
- Remember your **S.H.O.E.S.**
- Privately reflect
- Exercise patience
- Grow and move on

CHAPTER 3

COMMUNICATION

An amazing gift that initiates the journey of one mind to meet another.

Data or Delivery? Which is more important? Is communication more about *what* you say, or *how* you say it? It all depends on the context. Below are a couple of examples.

Scenario 1: A married couple is all dolled up for a formal dinner party and are pulling out of the driveway, headed to the big gala. Suddenly, the woman realizes that her corn silk shaded Corrina gown would go so much better with the off-white pearl earrings that her grandmother gave her—instead of the faceted chandelier earrings that she's currently wearing. She says, "Hang on a second. I want to go back and get the pearl earrings that my grandmother gave me."

The man pauses, and then patiently replies, "Are you sure honey? We're already running a little late. Remember, to kick off the festivities they're presenting you with that commendation for helping out with the fundraiser and coordinating the dinner party. And besides, you look fabulous!" *Delivery.*

Scenario 2: A couple is on a cruise ship. The husband is on the deck and the wife is in the cabin taking a nap when the ship begins to sink. The husband runs down and barges into the cabin, startling his wife out of a sound sleep and yells, "The ship is sinking! The ship is sinking! We gotta get outta here, lets go!

He grabs her by the hand, and they are halfway down the hallway when the wife says, "Hang on a second. I want to go back and get the pearl earrings that my grandmother gave me." But before she can get 'grandmother' out of her mouth, the man is screaming, "Are you <*bleepin*> crazy? Hell no! We're getting the <*bleep*> off this <*bleepin*> boat! C'mon!" *Data.*

In the first scenario, the husband's carefully worded dialogue is accented by his delivery. In the second scenario, delivery is a very noticeable factor, but it was the data posed that was of more significance. Is it the 'What' of a matter (data), or 'How' YOU say it (delivery) that is the better skill to have?

Communication as a whole is an immense topic with countless variations, endless definitions and immeasurable applications. It is so vast that even the self-proclaimed communication experts find it difficult to write about, and readers find it equally frustrating to learn more about. Research suggests that the overwhelming majority of all communication is non-verbal. [4] Does this imply we can tackle the topic of communication by just focusing on reading body language? Not a bad idea, but reading body language won't necessarily improve interpersonal communication skills, and has no bearing whatsoever on written communication. There is no escaping the importance of verbal communication. That means we all have to make a concerted effort toward developing better interpersonal communication, as in one-on-one dialogue.

Developing trustworthy verbal communication skills will not only enhance personal relationships, it will also facilitate greater cultural recognition and awareness between colleagues at work, which in the context of this book, is especially beneficial. We have to use email, memos, video conferencing, foreign language translation, and in some cases, even sign language with our customers, clients, co-workers, supervisors and subordinates.

While all the forms of interpersonal communication listed above are important, this chapter will focus on the LOUDEST communication that takes place.... The communication that we listen to the most.... The communication that we have a love/hate relationship with...namely the one-way communication that takes place in our minds: intrapersonal communication.

After twenty years of communicating with people from all over the world, with their many different cultural backgrounds, traditions and beliefs, under a myriad of emotionally compromising situations, I've come to believe that an attitudinal shift in *intrapersonal* communication (Me-talk) is the key to successful *interpersonal* communication (We-talk).

ME-TALK & WE-TALK

Timothy Gallwey in his book, *The Inner Game of Tennis, the Classic Guide to the Mental Side of Peak Performance,* talks about the two selves: Self-1 (the teller), and Self-2 (the doer). [5]

Self-1 is always judging YOU. Always criticizing YOU. Always telling YOU what YOU can't do. The communication from Self-1 is so loud and so constant, that we start to believe any and everything that Self-1 says about us. After some time our psychological self-defense mechanism kicks in and in order to protect our emotional psyche, we start to compare ourselves to other people by employing the same harsh evaluations of Self -1. This inner turmoil will soon manifest itself in your interpersonal communication with others. Cynicism will be apparent, pessimism rampant and the final outcome will be a reputation of hostility that breeds isolation, and even worse, prevents people from accurately gauging your competency. Negative Self-1 communication not only prompts disparaging judgments of YOU and your co-workers, it can also leave YOU suffering from a kind of workplace-aphasia.

Aphasia is the inability to comprehend written or verbal communication. The most devastating aspect of negative Self-1 communication, we'll refer to as *Me-talk,* is as a result of the constant bombardment of negativity YOU will be unable to accurately interpret any form of interpersonal communication, or *We-talk.* Both written and spoken communication will always be received with a hint of skepticism, or marred by a hue of gray, which, if left unchecked, will mark YOU as someone who is very difficult to deal with. It can become so matter-of-fact for YOU to receive and interpret information this way that everyone on the job will know it, except YOU.

Remember the foot pursuit from the opening chapter when I was parading my prisoner back to my police car and a couple of officers offered to give me a ride? Negative Me-talk convinced me that I had to prove I was worthy of my hire—that I was good enough to be on the police force. I thought to myself, *"What are they trying to say? That I need all this help to capture one bad guy?"* So when my partners offered to assist me, I blew them off—engulfed by my own misinterpretation of their offer to help me. Workplace-aphasia.

Self-2, on the other hand, is the "Doer." Free from the shackling confines of Self-1, Self-2 is about action. It doesn't suffer from the delusions of, "YOU are not good enough," or "That'll never work." Instead Self-2 says, "Don't try—Do." Self-2 helps to release our passions and desires to achieve goals. Begging to be trusted, Self-2 simply wants to engage...let's not *talk* about, lets *be* about.

I know it's embarrassing to admit that we've all fallen prey to Self-1, and even more troubling, at some point in our lives we've all told our own Self-2 to shut up! But here's the good news, by simply raising your awareness about the devastating effects of negative Me-talk, you're guaranteed to go to bed tonight a better YOU than the YOU who woke up this morning. As long as YOU are willing to make an attitudinal shift in your Me-talk communication, YOU can be well on the road toward quieting the damning perspectives of Self-1, and unleashing the action power of Self-2, thus enhancing your Me-talk and We-talk communication. Understand however, that without constant surveillance, eventually any negative Me-talk will slowly start to infect your We-talk. Make the shift and commit to it.

MAKING THE SHIFT

Whenever attempting to make an attitudinal shift, I hold best-selling author Seth Godin's concept on change in high regard. Godin says that when it comes to change, far too often people engage in hard paradigm shifts—whole scale changes of destruction and reconstruction.[6] Instead, Godin espouses soft innovation—subtle adjustments that make a tremendous difference. Attitudinal shifts are one of those things that greatly benefit from this concept. The balance of this chapter focuses on the three keys for changing your Me-talk and We-talk communication, thus improving your data, delivery and how YOU connect to the world.

Key 1: Negotiation. Change the way you view communication all together. Try to think of communication as a negotiation. Seek to establish grounds for an agreement, versus a stage to make declarations. Follow up questions such as, "Do you see what I'm saying?" is a declaration and can be less effective. Instead try, "What does my request mean to you?" The most valuable aspect of the communication is the "meaning." The vehicle used to deliver communication is a great deal less important than achieving the meaning of the message. Sometimes too much energy is expended on the vehicle of our communication, instead of focusing on the meaning of our message.

Key 2: Tone. Learning to use the proper voice inflection to communicate a particular point could take many years to master. It is truly an art form. However, a calm, measured voice tone that accents the highlight of your message not only makes a great impression, but it's appealing and attracts interest. (And of course avoid a monotone all together).

An inviting tone and any subsequent dialogue will always produce a higher level of comprehension. The greatest enemy to communication as a whole is interpretation, or the conception of another's message. Tones can play the most significant role in accurate interpretation of a message. If YOU say "I love working for ABC Company," with a sarcastic tone, it could mean that YOU actually hate working there. If YOU say the same thing in yet a different tone, it could mean that YOU truly enjoy being employed there. Tone helps to verify the meaning of your message and reduces the chances of misinterpretation.

Key 3: Exhibit Emotional Intelligence (EIQ). A wise man once told me that when it comes to communication there are only two things: people and problems. I paused for a moment at the sobering truth of his statement. I call this the "Inevitable Variable: People and Problems". No matter the industry, business, commercial enterprise or entrepreneurial endeavor, human communication will always include the variables of people and problems. And wherever there are people and problems, there are always emotions. So how can we combat the presence of the Inevitable Variable to be effective negotiators? By exhibiting Emotional Intelligence. **Emotional IQ** is the unique ability to reconcile your emotions and remain situationally alert when faced with a dilemma or challenge that requires making sound, ethical decisions.

DYNAMO ALERT!

*EIQ is an unparalleled glimpse into how well **you** manage **YOU**. It is an essential tool for effective communication. The most successful companies in the world covet employees with high EIQ. It is the one skill that will always make YOU more competitive than those without it. YOU need EIQ.*

Emotional Intelligence is developed over time, however, the first step in acquiring EIQ is understanding the concept of "getting past mad." The late Hall of Fame Coach Chuck Daily, who coached the world famous Men's Basketball Gold Medal winning team in the 1992 Olympics deemed the Dream Team, has been credited with coining the phrase "get past mad."

Whenever you've been arrested by your emotions, YOU do not have the ability to effectively negotiate nor the capacity to make a sound, ethical decision. Take a moment now and reflect; ask yourself if there's a past incident (personally or professionally) where had YOU not been so emotionally entangled, the outcome would have been much different—astronomically different? If YOU are like me, the answer is a resounding YES!

Author William Ury, Director of the Global Negotiation Project at Harvard University says, "The dangers of being reactionary is you lose sight of your interest"[7]. A clear, composed mindset will allow YOU to focus on the outcome of the negotiation, written or verbal. An attitude of negotiation, coupled with a calm, yet professional tone are trademarks of an individual with high EIQ.

Keep in mind, however, that negotiations are dynamic and very fluid. Try to think about negotiations as always *coming from,* or *going to* a place of clarity. Being situationally alert will prepare YOU for the hairpin turns of a negotiation, and will also help to monitor the pulse of the dialogue for the next potential place of clarity. YOU can never really learn to be a great negotiator, YOU can only learn as YOU negotiate.

DYNAMO PAK: "UPGRADING YOUR COMMUNICATIONS SKILLS"

Confidence. One of the quickest ways to upgrade your communication or negotiations skills is to add a heavy influx of confidence—a belief in YOU. The undercurrent that is masked in negative Me-talk is a lack of confidence. Be your biggest supporter, not your biggest fan. Fan is short for fanatic, and fanatics can be fickle and fair weather at times. The American sports culture breed fanaticism. Consequently, as is the case in the sports analogy, YOU will start to treat YOU in the same manner—upset and totally distraught when YOU "lose," and emotionally overjoyed when YOU "win." When it comes to your abilities, especially your communicative skills, don't be your biggest fan, be your biggest supporter. Support speaks of balance—not too high, and never too low. Support means celebrating your achievements great and small, while enduring the hardships of your less than stellar performances. Grant yourself grace when things don't quite turn out how YOU expected, and be quick to heap praise upon others during their times of contribution. Recognizing the efforts of other people will inspire YOU, and will help to re-assert your confidence. People are more apt to believe what YOU are saying if they feel that YOU are confident in YOU.

Communication Character. Another way to upgrade your communication skills is to recognize the character of your communication. Here's one of the most important requests that I make to participants in my role as a corporate trainer: Use a noun or adjective that most closely resembles your leadership style. Here is a list of some of the responses: eagle, support beam, water, mother bear, warrior, adaptable, and willing.

My years of training and experience have shown me that there is a direct correlation between people's leadership style and their communication style. Consequently, your communication embodies a particular type of character. If your leadership style is like an "eagle," your communication character may be like Spock of Star Trek—always surveying the variables and speaking unemotionally through logic. Or if your leadership style is like a "mother bear" or "warrior," your communication character may be like Wonder Woman, a feminist icon armed with the lasso of truth.

Media is a great recognition tool, and powerful teaching aid. Ask yourself, what character does my communication style most closely resemble? Use television and movie roles, or characters from a book, to help YOU recognize whom YOU most sound like. Continue to build the strengths of that style, but work very diligently to lessen the weakening effects of that style.

For instance, a "support beam" style of communicator would be great at negotiating an existing business relationship, but probably less effective for procuring new clients as users of this style are typically not bold. To upgrade their skills they could employ a technique called a "lukewarm contact," versus "cold calls." With a lukewarm contact, a support beam communicator can ask existing clients to facilitate a lunch meeting between them and one of their friends. The existing client could help ease the shyness the support beam communicator feels when dealing with strangers by sharing the highlights of their business relationship, thus encouraging the support beam communicator to assert their expertise. In this scenario, the strength of the support beam communicator is being showcased, while the area that may need improvement is being further developed.

Compose. Dr. J. Polansky argues that the most important verbal skill to possess is the skill of inquiry—the ability to ask questions.[8] I believe he has a legitimate point. And I'd like to extend his position by adding that I believe one of the most important verbal skills to have isn't a verbal skill at all, but the ability to write. This doesn't mean writing a message to be sent through correspondence or email, or meeting with someone and simply reading from a pre-written sheet of paper. I'm talking about writing a **Script**. Next time you have the opportunity to prepare for a meeting or negotiation use a Script. For example:

- Write down a vision of the desired outcome prior to the meeting;
- List the elements that are most beneficial for a successful outcome;
- Read it aloud, and role-play both sides of the proposed changes—empathizing with the possible perspective of your audience.

Here is an illustration of a Script regarding a proposal to change company policies:

Vision: *100% employee acceptance of proposed changes.*

Elements: *Effective communication of proposed changes*
                 Clear definitions of employee expectations
                 Evaluate effectiveness of proposed changes.

Topic/Subject: *Proposal for company policy changes.*

Audience communication culture: [Identify the most beneficial communication style of the audience, for example Baby Boomers, Gen Y, Millennials, etc.] _____

_____
_____
_____
_____.

Establish feedback loop: [Prior to message, make an announcement that feedback is desired for clarity.] ____

_____
_____
_____.

Data delivery: [With an intentional, yet welcoming tone announce to the audience the essence of the message with the use of the most advantageous delivery method – a heavy dose of facts, or comprehensive explanations.]

_____

_____

_____.

Create an atmosphere of negotiation, not a stage for declarations: [If possible, have the audience communicate to YOU in their own words what the message means to them. For example, people will have to submit to regulatory changes, however, if there is resistance regarding some other aspect of the message that has "wiggle room," establish two-way dialogue where the audience is now communicating to the speaker the essence of the message received, and the meaning of their (the audience) response. Being non-reactionary at this point is especially vital. Maintain a keen awareness of facial gestures and body language as well.] _____

_____

_____

_____

_____.

ROLE-PLAY TO FORECAST ISSUES AND PROVIDE ANTIDOTES:

[Operating assumptions are suppositions with high likelihoods of occurrence that facilitate communication. For example, based on American culture, I can make the operating assumption that most people reading this book have eaten a peanut butter & jelly sandwich. If YOU have dialogue with someone regarding possible snacks for your children, YOU are operating on the assumption that the person you're talking to knows what a PB&J sandwich is, and that it is often used as a snack option, so there's no need to explain it. The flow of our daily dialogue is facilitated based on making operating assumptions. When communicating a message, make some operating assumptions about which aspects of your message the audience will perceive as positive or negative. And in anticipation of that, verbally rehearse some mutually beneficial alternatives that can be discussed. Use a mirror or video camera during your rehearsals for added effectiveness. Remember, communication is a journey, not a destination.] ____

_____

_____

_____.

CHAPTER 4

OUTLOOK

The genesis of growth that graduates a narrow perspective to a much broader landscape of purpose.

*O*utlook is this book's first port of call toward enhancing YOU into a more dynamic YOU. This chapter initiates a subtle, yet very critical transition of focus in your reading experience – from *person* to *performer*. Your *person* foundation has already been laid in the previous chapters. YOU can now recognize the perils of justification (**Reflect**); the danger of motives (**Ethics**), and the crippling effect negative Me-talk can have on We-talk (**Communicate**). By the way, the awareness of this trio alone places YOU head and shoulders professionally above those without this foundation.

With what makes YOU tick finally in tow, we're ready to marry this intimate self-discovery of *person*, to the dynamo action

er. **Reflect, Ethics** and **Communicate** are
U as a person. **Outlook, Influence,** *and*
ntamount to YOU as a performer.

Chapter 2, the global participation in the so-
cial sciences of marketing strategy and competition renders us all
as performers. Merriam-Webster's dictionary defines the word
"perform" as: *to carry out an action or pattern of behavior.* Our
actions and behavior make up our performance. Whether YOU
are a subordinate, a manager, a supervisor, a leader, a professional athlete, or a parent, never forget we are all performers. In
any endeavor our performance is the signature of our lives, and
that bold signature is synonymous with the perception of who we
are. Reputation is the symbol of recognition that others attach
to YOU. Right or wrong, this label can follow YOU for the rest of
your life, so it is not something YOU should take lightly. YOU will
be remembered by how well, or how poorly, YOU perform. So lets
continue this dynamic enlightenment of YOU to ensure that when
YOU perform, YOU are recognized as being a top performer.

My thesis for becoming a top performer is best exemplified
from a single line in the 2009 British-American action mystery
film *Sherlock Holmes* starring one of my favorite actors. This actor's performances are vastly underrated, his genius is grossly
underestimated, and his passion and commitment for excellence
is often overlooked due to the ease and grace that he carries out
his magic on the screen. That actor is Robert Downey, Jr. That's
right, YOU heard me, Robert Downey, Jr. Oscar nominated, multiple Golden Globe Award winning and MTV Movie Award re-
cipient Robert Downey, Jr., whom I believe is one of the greatest

actors of our generation. When considering the level of his talent that stretches from *Chaplin* (1992) to *Tropic Thunder* (2008), RDII has single-handedly resurrected Hollywood from the ashes of failed superhero films over the past few years in his depiction of Tony Stark, aka *Iron Man*. Need I say more? (Okay, rant over).

In his portrayal of the famed investigator, Sherlock Holmes, Downey, Jr. visits the movie's main villain Lord Blackwood in a dark, cold and wet prison indicative of the late 1800s. Blackwood is scheduled for execution and has been remanded to a single person cell. Despite these less than desirable accommodations, Blackwood is calmly reading aloud from a book of black magic. Written on his cell walls are intricate drawings of witchcraft and devilment.

Blackwood's ominous reputation and callous demeanor has relegated prison staff to a kind of royal subservience to him. Holmes visits this brilliant miscreant at Blackwood's request. Immediately upon his arrival, Holmes interrupts Blackwood's reading and the two of them engage in a seemingly playful, albeit fast-paced, highly ingenious match of intellectual jousting complete with backhanded slights, innuendos and misdirection. Holmes' aim is to gauge Blackwood's involvement in the disappearance of five people, so for him the verbal skirmish is purposeful. Intensifying the pace of the dialogue in an effort to gain an advantage, as Holmes is prone to do, Holmes turns his back to Blackwood, lights up his trademark pipe and offers a scathing quip about Blackwood's imminent execution.

Blackwood, stuck behind bars, presses close to Holmes and said something that really caught my ear. He said, "*Holmes. You must widen your gaze. I'm concerned you underestimate the gravity of coming events."*

I knew immediately what the line meant to me as a professional development consultant. And I became excited to share the profundity of that statement with any performer who made the decision to become a top performer. So I say, "Performer. YOU *must widen your gaze.* I'm concerned that YOU under estimate the gravity of becoming a top performer."

TOP PERFORMERS

Becoming a top performer first begins with a decision. Henry Ford, founder of the Ford Motor Company has been quoted as saying, *"The man who says he can, and the man who says he can't are both right."* Performer, which one are YOU? If *you* say, "I can," then it is time to equip YOU.

STEP 1: LIBERATE YOUR PERSPECTIVE

Successful top performers widen their gaze by first liberating their perspectives. They release themselves from the hypnotizing effect of the rather mundane day-to-day operations of their job by engaging their minds in much broader enterprises or trends related to their occupation. They understand the value of consistent fundamental effort and can readily demonstrate a working knowledge of their job function, but their daily duties do not hold their minds captive.

Top performers also maintain a very high curiosity about cause and effect, whys and why nots, people and problems. Constantly investigating, they are very adaptive—forecasting issues before they become more serious problems, and providing solutions in advance for unlikely outcomes. Learning from these experiences, top performers seem to always be situationally alert.

STEP 2: BOLDLY OFFER IDEAS

Successful top performers widen their gaze by what they do when they identify a problem. When top performers identify a problem, they are not afraid to offer ideas for solutions. The fact of the matter is all solutions to problems come from an idea. Ideas give birth to knowledge. Knowledge leads to the application of an idea that eventually leads to a solution. Top performers understand that often a sound solution may be preceded by several failed attempts, so they do not suffer from what I call *Idea Indictment Syndrome.*

Idea Indictment Syndrome (IIS) occurs when an under-developed performer has the inability to separate the merits of their idea from their own personal honor. When there is constructive criticism of their idea, subconsciously, these performers view any analysis of their idea as a personal attack on their character and competency. Their hypersensitivity to the mere assessment of their idea is so intense that they gradually become over-protective, disagreeable and unable to intelligently respond to questions regarding the validity of their idea. Their dialogue is defensive and guarded, demonstrating a maternal instinct to protect their "baby" (idea) at all costs. Even in the face of better ideas.

Here is an example of IIS. A group is engaging in a brainstorming session. Someone in the group thinks of a solution to a problem, but they are unwilling to openly share their idea due to feelings of inadequacies. If the atmosphere is ripe for discussion, the reason for this self-imposed dismissal could mean that the performer is suffering from Idea Indictment Syndrome. What a performer suffering from IIS fails to realize is that *all ideas* go through the process of Idea Indictment. When an idea is presented to a group, from that point forward, the idea is going to be indicted, interviewed, interrogated, cross-examined, sentenced—"To Do" or "To Death" and then judged on levels of effectiveness.

IDEA INDICTMENT

Indicted—the idea is presented and will be gauged by a group of your peers for its usefulness.

Interviewed—the idea will be questioned by a group of your peers for greater understanding.

Interrogated—the idea will be openly criticized for its shortcomings.

Cross-examined—the idea will be critically analyzed and its merits debated by both supporters and naysayers.

Sentenced: The idea will be sentenced "To Do" (Implemented) or "To Death" (Terminated).

Judged: If the idea is implemented, it will be evaluated on its levels of effectiveness.

If the idea is purposeful it will withstand this test, even if it has to be modified. If it cannot be revamped and retried, it will be scrapped. This is the life cycle of an idea.

The onset of Idea Indictment Syndrome can occur at any time—during a brainstorming session, as well as the final stages of a project. Without training and professional development, IIS can lead to:

- Catastrophic meetings
- Overworked employees
- Unnecessary delays
- Loss of revenue
- Fractured business relationships and networking opportunities

The Idea Indictment process does not discourage top performers; in fact, top performers relish the opportunity to present multiple ideas to be tested.

DYNAMO ALERT!

Here's the secret that top performers employ to avoid suffering from IIS. Top performers fully understand the dilemma of blindly marrying themselves to any idea; so instead of placing a bull's eye on the sheer acceptance of their idea, they embrace the process of transforming that idea into knowledge. Knowledge provides the pathway to solutions, which leads to results. Top performers take aim at the results the idea will manifest, not the idea itself. (See Dynamo Pak).

STEP 3: TAKE ACTION

Top performers widen their gaze by taking action. And when they take action, their actions are strategic – more akin to chess, instead of checkers. Author John Stevens illustrates a story of a man who was standing on the bank of a very fast flowing river.[9] In that river he could see hundreds of people being swept along, struggling to keep from drowning. As each moment passes their numbers swell until there are thousands of people in the river, all gasping for air and shouting to the man on the bank to help them. What should he do? Dive in and help as many as he can? *Checkers.* Or does he run upstream and find out who is throwing them all in? *Chess.*

YOU may believe that a checkers move is the only ethical action the man on the bank should take, citing lives are at risk. Or YOU may believe that a checkers move in this instance is a waste of time, and that the situation demands a chess move to save more lives. Both have merit, but no matter which position YOU side with, T A K E   A C T I O N.

LET'S TAKE A CLOSER LOOK AT THIS ANALOGY IN TERMS OF 3 GROUPS:

Group 1: People continuously wade in and out of the river, tirelessly rescuing as many people as they possibly can. They believe that their actions are the only ethical actions to take. They are mortified that the other groups aren't helping them. People in Group 2 look as if they are about to help, then suddenly turn and run away. Can you imagine what Group 1 must have been thinking as they watched Group 2 leave? As members of Group 1 ponder for just a moment, the number of people in the river continues to swell, and the screams for help double so they dive back in. What do YOU think of Group 1's actions, checkers or chess?

Group 2: After briefly seeing the desperate attempts of Group 1, members in Group 2 find it too excruciatingly painful to watch people being plucked from the river one by one, while letting others perish. They can't understand why Group 1 isn't trying to find out the cause of this travesty. They decide it's best to go upstream to investigate the source of this horrific act and leave immediately. Group 2 tries to offer an explanation to Group 1, but there's little time for that. Group 2 takes off running up river, determined to find out the reason why so many helpless people are in the river. Can you imagine what Group 2 must have been thinking as they ran away from the bank of the river? Wondering if what they were doing was the ethical thing to do? Wondering what the other groups thought of them? Wondering what the people in the river thought of them? Running faster and faster upstream, members in Group 2 convince themselves to believe that in their heart-of-hearts, the potential loss of a few could help save a great many more. What do YOU think of Group 2's actions, checkers or chess?

Group 3: And then there's Group 3. These people do not believe that YOU should wade in and out of the river from the bank. That couldn't possibly be the best plan of action. YOU could be pulled down by any one of those hysterical people who are in fear of drowning, or be carried away by the fast moving current yourself. Group 3 do not believe that YOU should go up river, either.

Too many unknowns. Group 3 asks, "What if YOU are confronted with something that YOU don't know how to deal with?" In fact, Group 3 isn't exactly sure what to do...so they do nothing! And worse, they tell YOU to do nothing.

Now we can debate the merits of Group 1's actions, or the strategy of Group 2's plan, but what cannot be intelligently argued is Group 3's inaction. T A K E A C T I O N. In reality, it matters more that YOU took action of any kind, than whether the action was effective or not effective—chess or checkers.

When becoming a top performer liberate your perspectives, boldly offer ideas, and take action. There will be plenty of false starts, failed attempts, and relapses to your past train of thought. Under stress, we digress. But if YOU employ these steps your peers, supervisors and subordinates will start to take notice of your performance. And in no time at all, YOU will establish the reputation of being a top performer.

DYANAMO PAK: "HOW TOP PERFORMERS EFFECT CHANGE"

HOW TO EFFECT CHANGE

The boldness exhibited by most top performers is partly temperament, and partly homework. Research is critical. In order to effect change, educate yourself on the past history and culture of your company or team. Being better informed about the past journey of the group will guide YOU in offering ideas that are easier to digest in the future. Understand, however, that when merely making suggestions, or offering fresh perspectives it will often be perceived as YOU demanding that people change. Perception is reality when it comes to effecting change. Change, or even the mention of change without first considering the culture and traditions of a group, typically will not translate to full commitment.

It is difficult to introduce new ideas, or implement modifications to existing cultural norms without first cultivating the ground to receive the change. One way to cultivate the ground is to recognize the past achievements of those most responsible for the success of the agency. This is key: acknowledge both the people and their methods, and in doing so it will help to lower the defense mechanisms of the current personnel, making them more receptive to a new direction. This will also garner greater support from other individuals who weren't necessarily directly involved in the agency's current state, but whose minds have been shaped by that era. This public appreciation will open their minds for hearing your vision, and invite them to co-pilot the arrival of new changes.

HOW TO PRESENT AN IDEA

Presenting an idea begins with identifying a problem. To properly identify a problem, whenever possible try to create a model of the problem or challenge. Author Dr. Peter A. Rogerson offers an elementary, yet brilliant definition for a model:

Models are a device for simplifying realities so that the relationships between variables may be more clearly studied.

It has been my experience that the "relationship between variables" is one of the best places to begin your problem analysis. You'll be amazed to discover that often times the variables Dr. Rogerson is speaking of are totally oblivious to how many other sections they're related to, and equally unaware of how they positively or negatively affect those related sections. The under appreciation of linkage, or how concepts and efforts of one section can effect the operations of another, is where YOU should concentrate your focus, and brainstorm ideas that:

- Raise linkage awareness between sections—intra and interdepartmentally
- Raise questions about current methods—seeking to utilize soft innovations
- Raise alternatives that promote efficiency—which in turn, saves money or makes your agency money

Now that YOU have properly identified a problem and are ready to offer an idea, here's how YOU do it.

Step 1: Determine if YOU are still in the brainstorming stage, or ready to move to the idea presentation phase. Brainstorming ideas cannot answer some of the basic inquiries of the idea such as overall objective, budget impact, or resource pool. Ideas that are ready to be presented, however, are capable of addressing most preliminary issues, and can be implemented on a low level with immediate measurable effect. Ensure that your idea has an edge over other competing ideas before presenting it. Research, practical experience and Idea Indictment can help with this determination.

Step 2: Self-evaluate. Once you're ready to present your idea, ask yourself, "Do I have a professional objective, or am I emotionally entangled with this idea?" Frustration along with a whole host of other emotions often accompany the recognition of a problem, so the strong desire to implement a quick-fix is natural. Force yourself to take a step back from the situation. Self-awareness and emotional IQ are vital – even before YOU share your idea with your most trusted colleague.

Step 3: Performers often believe they need to have an answer for every single argument against their idea, but this isn't entirely true. Ideas remain in a developmental state for much of their existence – up to and including implementation. So for Step 3, once your idea has been adequately presented at the right time with the right audience, cut the umbilical cord. Re-direct your focus towards further developing any modifications to your original idea, or be prepared to leapfrog to a better idea if one is presented. Defending the vulnerabilities of your idea is not an act of valor. And getting on the bandwagon of a newer idea isn't abandonment. A good idea will stand on its own merit despite any glaring deficiencies or initial resistance.

Step 4: Lastly, once management has made their final decision on how they're going to proceed, execute the new idea or change with passion. How YOU respond after presenting an idea that was not accepted, or rejected for another one is essential to your professional development. Your dutiful execution of the new direction is an act of professionalism that is the trademark of a top performer and will play a major role regarding the acceptance of any future ideas from YOU.

As YOU can see, presenting ideas are essential for business continuity and production. Do not be intimidated by the humbling beginnings of an idea—it is simply raw data. In actuality, all ideas begin as raw data. Professor Jerry Ratcliffe of Temple University in Philadelphia implies that raw data can be meaningless, unless it can be attributed to a cause or effect or lead to more productive thought processes—only then can it be enhanced to the level of information. Once the information is shared, and can be exercised, it can then become knowledge.[11] Knowledge offers the power to apply the idea, and it is the application of knowledge that produces the results that top performers strive for, not the thankful recognition and acceptance of their idea.

HOW TO REBOUND FROM A "FAILED IDEA"

Failed ideas are part of the solution. Solutions to challenges come by way of "failed ideas." The Wright Brothers had "failed ideas" enroute to the first airplane. Thomas Edison had "failed ideas" that eventually lead to the first light bulb. Little known David Crosthwait, electrical and mechanical engineer who has been credited with 39 U.S. patents and 80 foreign patents for his inventions in heating ventilation, air conditioning, and refrigeration processes—had "failed ideas."

In my role as a training consultant, one of the first things that I do when working with a company is a "**Trash Run**." I take a look at what a particular department has thrown away. More times than not, a "failed idea" lay on the cutting room floor or in the trash bin. One key to rebounding from a failed idea is to determine if, in fact, the idea wasn't helpful for creating a solution in the first place. As I've reiterated earlier, YOU have to do your research, but determine if the trash run doesn't already include solutions.

Another method that YOU can utilize that is especially helpful in rebounding from a "failed idea" is to be a "failed idea cupid"— play matchmaker of the "failed ideas" to discover if there were some good qualities from one that could be great if matched with another idea. Also determine if these "failed ideas" actually had the proper backing needed to accurately assess their usefulness. This is key. Often time's people have great ideas that are saddled with half-hearted efforts by personnel, which can lead to failure and confusion. Exhaust every lead YOU develop from the trash run.

Lastly, here's the silver lining YOU can benefit from when rebounding from a "failed idea" – document the "failure." At some point top performer YOU will compete for a promotion, and YOU can use the past experience of a "failed idea" to your advantage. Employers will always be interested in hearing how YOU were able to correct the negative consequences of a bad situation by either lessening the damage of the "failure," or how it lead YOU to learn an invaluable lesson that raised your overall level of expertise. By documenting the particulars, several things come into play at this point. One, YOU signal to the employer that YOU are willing to admit a mistake and that humility is a part of your character. Two, YOU demonstrate resourcefulness on how YOU created a solution to a major problem. Now the employer knows that *when* something goes wrong, they can trust that YOU won't handcuff yourself to a bad idea and swallow the key (IIS), that when YOU readily identify problems YOU will take action, and that YOU have the ability to provide strategic **Outlook** for solutions.

CHAPTER 5

INFLUENCE

The romantic relationship between knowledge and action that compels a response sparked by passion or duty.

Possessing the ability to be influential has traditionally been viewed as a natural gift. The perception is that these gifted people are almost mystical, capable of rendering someone helpless against their undeniable powers of persuasion. I disagree. I believe influence can be acquired by the simple recognition of present day behavior, which creates an effect that compels future conduct from others.

CASE IN POINT:

Kerry was a pretty woman by almost anyone's standard, and it only took a few minutes of conversation with her to see that brains accompanied her beauty. She attended one of the largest universities in the country and worked part time in the campus bookstore. I remember the first time I met Kerry. It was two o'clock in the afternoon and the weather was sunny and gorgeous. I was a street cop on routine patrol when a candy apple red Mercedes convertible ran a stop sign right in front of me. Once Kerry recognized her mistake, she was halfway in the intersection. She and I were looking eye-to-eye as she sank down into her seat apologetically, and slowly crept through the intersection.

Anticipating being stopped, Kerry pulled over immediately. I activated my overhead lights and approached her vehicle. She was incredibly embarrassed and equally frustrated with herself as she rambled on and on with a mixed bag of apologies and personal reprimands. Her chatter finally culminated with her handing me a driver's license as she softly banged her forehead on the steering wheel repeatedly in disgust. I told her to wait there and that I'd be back with her in a minute. She mentioned very early on that she was looking for the university and that she was new to the city. Though the university was one of the largest in the country, college kids often found themselves on the east side of University Avenue, instead of the west side of the highway where the campus was actually located. I wasn't much of a ticket writer so I did what I usually did in situations like that, I issued her a written warning. Besides, dope hounds have bigger fish to fry.

When I informed Kerry that she would be receiving a warning, her beautiful green eyes lit up as she took back her license and practically yelled a dozen "thank-yous" to me as I walked back to my patrol unit. Seconds later, I was back on the hunt.

A couple of weeks later after shift change, it was about one-thirty in the morning when I decided to make my first of many patrols of Fair Oaks Projects. The locals called it "Unfair Oaks." The Fair Oaks Projects was a state-sponsored housing development in my district that had a long-standing reputation for drive-by shootings, narcotics sales and prostitution. Cops had been arresting people in Fair Oaks since I was in grade school. The east entrance to Fair Oaks was at the bottom of a hill so I used the glide technique for sneaking up on late night loiterers by turning off my headlights, cutting the engine, putting the patrol car in neutral and coasting down the hill unannounced.

As I coasted down, everything appeared relatively normal. There was the neighborhood drunk that everybody loved, a couple of veteran prostitutes who waved as I coasted by, and a homeless guy walking down the street. When I made it to the bottom of the hill, I turned on my engine and lights and was about to drive away when I saw a candy apple red Mercedes convertible parked right in front of the east gate to the projects. Before driving away I paused for a moment, squinting as I stared at the car. "Where have you seen that car before?" I asked myself. I knew I had stopped that car but I just couldn't remember. Overcome by curiosity, I decided to investigate further.

I exited my patrol car and approached the vehicle. The convertible top of the Mercedes was up, but I could see that there were people in it. I shined my flashlight into the car and to my surprise it was Kerry. Though she was initially startled, Kerry was excited to see me. She rolled down her window and said, "Oh hey! Hi Officer Lane, how are you?" Then she quickly turned to her roommate who was sitting in the front passenger seat and said, "This was the cop I was telling you about." Turning back to me she smiled widely and asked again, "How are you?"

I told her that I was fine, and then I asked her what she was doing in this part of town at this time of night.

Kerry pointed to the back seat passenger and said, "We're giving him a ride home."

Emerging from the backseat was a fine looking young man who looked like an athlete at first glance. He respectfully introduced himself, shook my hand and told me that his mother lived in apartment #3251. He also stated that he was raised in Fair Oaks and had earned a football scholarship from the university. He was the starting tail back and invited me to a game.

He said, "Look for number 34", as he strolled up to the apartment.

My partner arrived on scene to check on me as I said goodbye to the group.

"College kids?"

"Yep," I replied.

"Figures. No car like that is from around here," he said.

I thanked him for the back-up and then went back in service.

Over the summer I would periodically see Kerry's car parked in front of apartment #3251, and later discovered that she and the football player were dating. Later that fall, I was at the police sub-station when I was handed a B.O.L.O. (Be on the lookout) sheet. It said that a couple of day's prior, police were in pursuit of a red convertible Mercedes that was last spotted at the university. Officers lost sight of the vehicle, but it was later located near the

Fair Oaks Projects. When officers approached the Mercedes, an unidentified male was seen sitting in the driver's seat counting a large roll of money with a gun in his lap. When he realized that it was the police that were confronting him, the subject fled the scene leading police on a second pursuit. During this pursuit, the unidentified subject caused several collisions, one of which critically injured a citizen. He also rammed a police unit, and threw the gun and crack cocaine out of the window before getting away yet again.

After reading it, my partner and I both looked up at each other at the same time as the sergeant continued rattling off a long laundry list of departmental policies and other boring announcements. I wondered if it was Kerry's car and her boyfriend. After show-up, I ran the license plates myself, and sure enough, it was Kerry's car!

I'm not exactly sure why, but I couldn't wait to give her a stern lecture about this situation, and it wasn't long after I got that chance. A couple hours after hitting the street, I saw Kerry walking around Fair Oaks looking distraught. She flagged me down and told me that her boyfriend borrowed her car and hadn't brought it back all weekend. I updated Kerry on the latest events regarding her car and told her that it would probably be a good idea for her to contact her parents and let them know what happened.

Initially, she repeatedly shook her head "no" as she began to cry. But I gave her that "c'mon-on-now" look and she said okay. Then I ordered her not to come over to Fair Oaks at night, or during the day for that matter.

She asked desperately, "What about my car?"

"I'll find your car. You just focus on school. And don't come back over her. Deal?"

Kerry begrudgingly answered, "Deal...I guess".

My warning fell on deaf ears. The very next weekend, my partner stopped a car driven by one of the neighborhoods better-known thugs, and located in the backseat was Kerry and her roommate. As I arrived on scene to back-up my partner, I was shocked to see Kerry in the vehicle. I immediately tore into her, admonishing her for ignoring my orders. But she cut me off, and exploded with an expletive laced tirade that would make even a sailor blush. Then, to top it off, she laughed about it. I was stunned. I couldn't believe it. Was this the same college kid who I met in the summer? What had gotten into her? I looked more closely at her, specifically her eyes. Could it be? No way! Was Kerry....high?

Any further interactions would've only antagonized her and worsened the situation, so I stepped back and allowed my partner to handle the stop. Once they drove away, I turned to my partner in disbelief when he said, "Looks like the crack monster got your girl." His words echoed in my mind. He was one of the most respected cops in the city and taught me everything I knew about narcotics interdiction. There was no denying what he said. I was speechless.

Over the next few months I watched this beautiful, intelligent young woman, full of potential and promise—deteriorate to a skin and bones streetwalker who became instantly enraged every single time she saw me. What I found so confusing was why she seemed to direct her venomous attacks only at me, while appeasing every other cop who dealt with her. We had become so adversarial that I once told her that if she so much as flicked a cigarette butt on the ground that I would take her to jail for littering. She just turned her back and walked away as she offered me the world famous one-finger salute.

Late one night, or should I say early morning, as fate would have it, I "glided" down to a car parked at the bottom of the hill near the east gate of Fair Oaks. It was an out-of-towner in a rental car who was soliciting company with Kerry. They were so engrossed in their conversation neither one of them saw this large white police car barreling right at them. I was able to get out on them very quickly and I could clearly see that Kerry was trying to conceal something in her left hand. Suspecting that it was drugs, I seized her hand and the fight was on! In short order my partner, who had approached on foot from the opposite direction, was covering the driver while I worked intentionally not to hurt Kerry, but secure what I suspected to be crack in her hand.

After placing her in handcuffs, my suspicions were confirmed. Kerry had a small, in fact a very small piece of crack cocaine. It was barely enough to classify for the lowest level of arrest—the equivalent to a speeding ticket, but it was an opportunity for me to get her off the street and a chance at rehab.

When I placed her in the backseat of my patrol car, Kerry was almost demonic in her profane, abusive rebuke of me – ranting and raving, and eventually kicking out the back window of my unit. While my partner read the out-of-towner the riot act and released him, I began inventorying the contents of Kerry's purse as she hurled insult after insult at me. Inside were the usual contents: brillo pad, crack pipe, a small wire used to scrape off the residue from inside the pipe, and a cell phone.

Thinking that the cell phone might be stolen I flipped it open to see the call log. At the top of the call history was a number titled "Mom & Dad." Although it was 3:00 a.m., I took a chance that it was Kerry's parents and called the number.

A woman's voice groggily answered the phone. "Hello, Mrs. Winn? Do you have a daughter named Kerry?"

"Yes, yes I do. Is she okay?"

I laid it on thick, "This is Officer Lane. My apologies for the early hour ma'am, but I've just arrested your daughter for narcotics paraphernalia and I want you to listen to something." I placed the phone to the back window of the patrol car and allowed Kerry's mother to hear for herself the devastation that had consumed her daughter. It was cruel, but I wanted to shock her mother's system. Too often I've seen an addict convince their loved ones that they're not dependent, only to set them up for a painful cycle of abuse.

Mrs. Winn was still reeling from disbelief as I shared with her how I met Kerry and how we came to this culminating point. I concluded the conversation by saying; "I can take her to jail or to the airport. Which would you rather I do"?

By this time Mr. Winn was listening on the phone and immediately chimed in, "Please! Take her to the airport."

My partner was looking at me with eyes as wide as saucers and mouthed the words, "Are you <bleepin> nuts?"

I waived him off and turned my back. I said to them, "I'll get her home."

Kerry heard the last of my conversation with her parents. She was reduced to tears and simply sat in the backseat of my patrol car and wept. Meanwhile, I had to try and fulfill my end of the bargain. After speaking with my superiors and receiving a thirty minute butt chewing, I was allowed to take Kerry to the bus depot, but only after she sobered up. I took her to a hospital closest to the bus station and sat with her for the next six hours while I completed my paperwork. When Kerry was finally sober we had just eighteen minutes to catch the next Greyhound bus headed to a little city outside of Des Moines, Iowa.

With no handcuffs on, Kerry slowly followed me out of the emergency room. We probably looked like an odd couple to the people in the waiting area. I opened the front passenger side door of my patrol unit and she got in. She just stared out the window. I wasn't quite sure what to say, so we sat in silence during the short ride to the bus station. Once there, I retrieved her pre-purchased ticket and reached out to give it to her. I simply said, "You're free to go. All you have to do is get on that bus, and you'll be fine."

Kerry seemed anxious. Fighting back tears, she paused for a moment, looking back and forth at the ticket and the bus. Then she snatched the ticket out of my hand and boarded. I have to admit that I was hurt and confused by her lack of gratitude. Trying to cope, I told myself as I drove back to the police station barely awake, "You did the right thing, kiddo. You did the right thing". Little did I know how loud those words would ring true.

Several years later, I received a call from my baby brother. Well at 6' 5" he wasn't much of a baby, but he was my little brother nevertheless. I could tell by the sound of his voice something was terribly wrong. He told me that his roommate had been found murdered in their apartment. He said that he had been out of town at a basketball tournament and was about an hour away. After several back-and-forths about whether he was joking or not, I asked him what he was going to do. Very dejectedly he said that he was going back to his apartment to get some clothes and figure out where he was going to stay. I inadvertently blurted out, "Don't go there. That's a murder scene!"

DOING THE RIGHT THING

"Acorn, (his nickname for me) I can't borrow just anybody's clothes...they won't fit."

He was right, so I told him to come to my place and we'd figure something out. He agreed, as I nervously awaited his arrival. This was a sticky situation—someone was murdered while the roommate was conveniently out of town, and the roommate's brother is a cop. Was it possible that I would have to turn my own brother over to the authorities? What would he say when he got to my place? What if he admitted to me that he did it? What the heck would I do then?

Seeking guidance I contacted a good friend of mine who was assigned to the homicide division. Detective Garcia was one those cops who didn't get much fan fair, but those who worked with him knew of his integrity, work ethic and competency. He commanded the respect of his peers and supervisors. He also took a personal interest in me, encouraging me to test for rank of Detective. He saw first hand the talent and skill that I demonstrated as a street cop, and said to me, "Officer Lane, you could stay at your current level and fall in love with yourself everyday, or promote to greater challenges and responsibilities." I would later accept the challenge.

I called Det. Garcia and shared my dilemma with him. He told me to wait by the phone while he made some calls. Evidently there had been two homicides that day, one on the south side and one on the north side. The one related to my brother was the latter. I sat there nervously awaiting the arrival of my brother, and direction from Det. Garcia. It was the longest fifty-two minutes of my life!

Finally, there was a knock at the door. I opened the door and could immediately sense the pain on my brother's face. He was hurt. The instep of the door jam put us eye to eye, so I said to him, "I gotta know...?"

He quietly, but confidently looked at me and said, "No, 'Corn."

Now more confident than ever of his innocence, I hugged my baby brother and invited him inside. When I received a call back from Det. Garcia I told him that my brother was with me and to help eliminate any conflict of interest, we were going to contact a lawyer. Detective School 101 says that my brother would be listed as a suspect, so it was a fundamentally correct move. Det. Garcia agreed, and I started making some calls to find my brother a competent and affordable defense attorney.

I discovered very quickly that the words "competent," "affordable" and "attorney" are not compatible. When I did come across a lawyer's office that was empathetic to our plight, the same name kept coming up of the individual who they would call if they were in the same pinch—Jake "J.A." Alexander. He was also known by his nickname, "Bulldog." I contacted J.A. and was turned away immediately by his secretary when she informed me that J. A. charged $5,000 just to take a look at a case! Though discouraged, I continued to search for competent counsel for my brother.

Several moments later, my phone rang. To my disbelief the man on the line was J.A. himself. He asked me if I knew a girl by the name of Kerry Winn. I thought for a minute, Kerry Winn... Kerry Winn. Oh, the college girl from Iowa!

"Yes sir, Mr. Alexander. I know a young woman named Kerry Winn."

He said, "Kerry Winn is my goddaughter. I bought her that Mercedes as an early college graduation gift. I know what you did for her. She's doing a lot better, but she hasn't completely conquered her addiction. Come by my office in the morning. I'll take a look at your brother's case, and if he's innocent I'll represent him for free until it goes to trial."

Unbelievable! And true to the reputation that preceded him, "Bulldog" commanded the respect of the investigators and in short order; they eliminated my brother as a suspect and soon after that found the killers.

After all was said and done, I had lunch with J.A. and discovered that he knew more about me than just the way I handled his goddaughter. He knew that I wrote professional, objective police reports, had the admiration of my peers, earned the respect of the thugs in my district, and in his words, "...played in a dirty game, fair and ethically." This wasn't a mere case of returning a favor. Recognizing how I carried myself everyday influenced J.A.'s decision to help me. There was no magical potion that I used to coerce him, or some Jedi mind trick that left him defenseless against my request for legal assistance. He simply recognized my name, and believed in what I demonstrated daily which evoked a response from him far and above the norm. That kind of response occurs when there is recognition of a present day deed, which creates an effect that compels a response from others in the future. It's called an *ECHO*.

ECHO

Being influential is about YOU engaging in what I call *"Everyday Everyway Ethics"* – necessary ingredients that make up an ECHO. Making the daily choice to be ethically sound in your decision-making will establish the foundation of your ECHO. YOU build upon that foundation by exhibiting conduct that is a reflection of moral principles, and by demonstrating respect for your fellow man. These values strengthen your ECHO. An ECHO is so strong, that it can influence your supervisors, your peers, your subordinates and even powerful decision makers outside your arena of performance. The interesting thing about an ECHO is when the professional YOU makes a statement, the sound wave of your ECHO speaks on your behalf repeatedly—and YOU don't have to say a word.

DYANAMO PAK: "LEVERAGING YOUR ECHO FOR MAXIMUM EFFECT"

HOW TO LEVERAGE YOUR ECHO

In order to maximize your contributions, YOU need to leverage your ECHO. The method for leveraging a far-reaching ECHO is modeling. Your ECHO should model the following three key characteristics – Motivation, Mastery and Might.

For those of us who have kids (or who are still kids at heart) we've all seen the commercials that advertise a really neat toy that has all the children in the room going "oooo & ahhh." The stunt scenes that highlight the toy's abilities are often over exaggerated, but it looks so cool we overlook the reality. Then after stirring the room with excitement, the commercial concludes with the phrase: "Batteries not included. Some assembly required." One of these two statements can always be said of YOU. And one of these statements should never be said about your ECHO.

MOTIVATION: BATTERIES NOT INCLUDED

ECHO Rule #1: Never allow a boastful misinterpretation of YOU to be falsely advertised; and Rule #2 make it is nearly impossible for it to be said of YOU, "Batteries not included." Here's why, your battery is motivation—intrinsic motivation. YOU are motivated from something that comes from within *you*, something that is unaffected by outside circumstances. It is part of your devotion to an ethical standard that is greater than YOU.

It is your *"Obedience to a truth...(Reflect)"* that prevents YOU from taking shortcuts and drives YOU to completion. It is your *"... faith in a greater good (Ethics)"* that energizes YOU in moments of fatigue. You're motivated to do what YOU do simply because it's the *just* thing to do—with or without an audience. Therefore, "Batteries not included" never applies to anyone with an ECHO.

MASTERY: SOME ASSEMBLY REQUIRED

Your ECHO will clearly demonstrate your work ethic and silence any critics who say of YOU "Batteries not included". YOU won't advertise things that YOU can't do – only skills that YOU can perform on demand. However, let it be said of YOU until the cows come home "Some assembly required." In order to leverage your ECHO for service YOU have to master your chosen field. That means continuous learning, continuous study and continuous professional development. The late, great teacher and author Dr. Howard Hendricks wrote, *"When you stop learning...you start dying."*[12] It should always be said of YOU, "Some assembly required", but only because YOU constantly strive to increase your capacity to learn, and gain greater insight toward mastering your profession. The mastery of any skill is greatly enhanced by consistently setting new goals, once old goals have been successfully realized.

HERE ARE THREE SIMPLE STEPS FOR SETTING A GOAL:

Step 1: Choose an accountability partner, and then make your goal a public matter, not a private one. Taking a cue from my pistol competition-shooting mentor, 4-time United States Practical Shooting Association Grand Master Yong Lee, YOU have to demonstrate what's called **championship humility**. Championship humility is a mentality that outwardly expresses your refusal to be restrained by the fear of failure, or be discouraged by the possibility of disappointment. Championship humility says YOU only see failure in not trying. Fear is felt, but not acted upon. Disappointment is acknowledged, but not focused on. The focus is on the process to realize the goal – despite the emotions we sometimes feel that are contrary to the goal. That's the heart and mind of a champion. So YOU humbly, yet publicly, declare your goal and YOU risk being laughed at, ridiculed or even humiliated to be *successful*.

DYNAMO ALERT!

YOU define success. Accomplishing goals is not for others to define. Having an accountability partner who will be open and honest with YOU is vital when reaching for a goal, as is the support that comes from a group. But YOU, and YOU alone define whether the effort to obtain the goal was successful.

Step 2: Write down a bullet list of your action plan. Just one or two words of each task in your plan so that YOU know what it means. Then post it in multiple places that are visible—i.e. desk, workspace, screensaver, sun visor, bathroom mirror and of course, ol' faithful, the refrigerator. YOU want to create an atmosphere where YOU are being constantly reminded of your action plan, not necessarily the goal. Here's why. Because there are so many variations and definitions of success, goals are often redefined during the process to attain them. For **Step 2**, a laser-like focus and commitment to the *process* of reaching for the goal is significantly more important to your professional development than the actual goal itself.

Step 3: Categorize your goals by using one of the following three levels of success. The first level of success is Soul Success. Soul Success is a party of one—YOU. YOU celebrate what YOU define as successful. It is your own private experience and revelation that YOU **Reflect** upon. Some of the greatest personal gains to be made happen at this level of success.

The second level of success is Stored Success. Stored Success is when YOU celebrate with your accountability partner the journey experienced during your *attempt* to reach the goal—while being mindful that the full manifestation of the goal is still in Store. Accomplishing the goal may be temporarily placed on hold because of a desire to start a family, a move to another state or even a big promotion, but YOU fully intend to reinitiate the process of achieving the goal. Understand, however, Stored goals have an expiration date. 'Life' will eventually overtake YOU, so be mindful of how long YOU allow those goals to remain in storage.

And the third level of success is Splash Success. When YOU fully realize any goal, Splash Success is to be celebrated with anyone who cares about YOU. Family and friends who supported YOU, or anyone YOU can positively influence to set a goal of their own, make them wet with success by sharing your testimony!

Notice any similarities between the varying levels of success? Yes, YOU define success, and the final outcome for realizing any goal is celebration.

MIGHT: INVESTMENT

Lastly, leverage your ECHO with all of your Might! Fact: YOU will never know how much of an impact YOU have on people. Constantly scan those around YOU because one day YOU may need to disciple them. Wrap your mind around this top performer—there are people out there who, for whatever reason, can only be influenced by YOU. There'll be something about YOU that easily connects with them, where others have tried and failed. It is your obligation to invest in them because someone invested in YOU. Guide, mentor and train them to the very best of your abilities. Share with all your Might! the gifts that '**you & YOU**' possess with anyone who asks, and ensure that they are edified, encouraged and effective. YOU may not feel that you're worthy to train or teach anyone, but YOU must do it. There isn't a formula on exactly what to do, so I ascribe to Amelia Earhart who said it best, "*The most effective way to do it, is to do it.*"

CHAPTER 6

LEADERSHIP

A concert of submission and service that co-governs effort between forerunner and follower.

Your desire to exist with a heightened state of renewal motivated YOU to become more aware of how the environment has shaped your perspective: **Reflect.** Your obedience to truth that enhances your fellowship with humanity has been adopted and will serve as the ambassador for your actions: **Ethics.** You seek to negotiate, rather than declare, and now fully understand that unhealthy Me-talk can poison healthy We-talk: **Communicate.** With the foundation of your *person* established, YOU widened your gaze so that YOU can maximize your *performance* with strategic purpose: **Outlook.** YOU can now identify the power of your ECHO, and can compel a passionate response from others: **Influence.**

All of these characteristics help make YOU very influential. Now that YOU have influence, what should YOU do with this new professional capacity? How should anyone handle the compelling force of being influential?

DYNAMO ALERT!

*Once YOU have acquired the capacity to be influential, there are only two things influence can be used for—to serve YOU, or to serve others. **Lead**.*

Being influential can champion a cause for the betterment of a group, or it can be a Pandora's box of hidden evils aimed solely at personal gain. I won't bore YOU with an endless list of news stories over the past decade depicting self-serving men and women that range from politicians to elementary school teachers who have made mortifying decisions and set shameless examples on how to yield their influence. There's a safe bet that at the moment you're reading this chapter the media is following such an incident. However, it is my belief that once someone has achieved the ability to be influential, they have an enormous responsibility to serve someone other than themselves. They have a responsibility to model, inspire, guide and direct those whom they impact, and those who consider them a role model. Modeling, inspiring, guiding and directing are all definitive characteristics of leadership.

There are many different philosophies about leadership, and probably an equal number of leadership styles, but there are two basic methodologies: one is leadership through the *power* of a title, and the other is leadership through the *persuasion* of influence. The focus in this book has been the latter.

YOU are a leader. YOU do not need the title of Owner, CEO, Vice President or Senior Management, in order to be a leader or have influence. In fact, research has shown that peers and immediate supervisors have the greatest impact on influencing employee behavior from a leadership standpoint. What YOU *do* need to be an effective leader is a willingness to submit yourself to the process of apprenticeship. YOU must be willing to serve and study under a leader who demonstrates an intelligent, ethical approach to challenges, and has a perspective that is both broad and strategic. Within these pages I'll equip YOU with a few areas of concentration, but YOU must submit yourself to an apprenticeship. It is during your apprenticeship that your skillsets will be enhanced tremendously.

FOLLOWERSHIP

You haven't stopped reading, so I'll assume YOU have a desire to use your influence to lead others. But first, I have a few pertinent questions to ask YOU about your desire...not to lead, but to follow:

- How badly do YOU want to be a follower?
- Do you know what it takes to be a follower?
- Are followers born, or are they made?
- What are some of the better-known followership theories?

These questions may seem confusing to YOU – follower inquiries in a leadership chapter? After all, if someone were asked, "Do you want to be a follower?" they would probably respond with a resounding "NO!" It's been drilled in our heads as far back as we can remember, "Don't be a follower." Yet the evolution of great leadership derives from willful and intentional followership.

Followership can be defined as: being voluntarily submitted to the service of someone who carries a vision that you can also perceive, and the full manifestation of that vision is something that you wholeheartedly believe.

Followership under the tutelage of an authentic leader will prime YOU for service at the leadership level. The time spent under their guardianship will help to establish your personal foundation and shape your professional **Outlook**. The sheer volume of learning that takes place during this kind of apprenticeship is mind numbing, with too many topics to discuss in this single volume. However, once YOU have been elevated to a position of leadership, and embrace this extraordinary opportunity, there is one aspect of leading people that I believe is the best-kept secret for great leadership. Once mastered, this unique skill can launch YOU to unimaginable heights as a leader. It's the art of accessing *discretionary effort*.

DISCRETIONARY EFFORT

To define the significance of discretionary effort, I must first shed light on the term professional development. By most accounts the technical definition of professional development revolves around the enhancement of knowledge, abilities and skills for a given profession. Many private and public sector agencies lament professional development as their primary means for employee training and advancement, but for most of these institutions the traditional form of professional development is merely a mirage.

Most corporate training programs that prepare employees to meet the needs of the company do not engage in a traditional form of professional development (apprenticeship), but instead employ very clever checklists and protocols that give the impression of competency. It isn't admitted in an open forum, but decision-makers on the highest levels of these organizations are typically in favor of using this strategy to train employees and even first line supervisors in the name of uniformity and efficiency. Whether an individual is working at the drive-thru window of a fast-food restaurant, or the lobby of a national bank, a checklist form of professional development does allow employees to meet the minimum requirement of their job function on a satisfactory level. But these employees are often without problem-solving skills, resourcefulness or the ability to generate ideas for solutions. They just simply adhere to their checklist. And when confronted with a challenge that presents itself outside the scope of that checklist, their response becomes very defensive in nature, or even argumentative. Their final response is to retrieve another person who may or may not have the aforementioned capacities indicative of a highly skilled practitioner. The unfortunate outcome results in an organization populated with "dumb-downed" robots, underdeveloped personnel, and a sea of untapped potential.

Now before I shout too loudly from high upon my soapbox, it should be noted that effective corporate leadership should reserve critical decision-making to just a few key individuals who possess those skill sets. But there are hidden gems of human energy, increased productivity, innovative ideas and sound solutions residing in many individuals who've become stagnant, suppressed by a poor managerial environment, or who have not been properly developed – trapped by today's version of professional development (checklist). Secreted within some of these followers are priceless reserves of energy and capacity called discretionary effort.

Discretionary effort is the concealed pocket of very powerful dynamo that a person possesses, enabling them to perform exceedingly above their given job description – thus maximizing their full potential. Access to this gold mine of human capital is granted voluntarily by the follower, and typically only to leaders with whom the follower shares a genuine connection. This connection is the basis of the follower' response. When leader and follower are confronted with a challenge, based on their relationship, there are three levels of follower responses, which have three very different outcomes.

- The first level of follower response occurs when a leader diagnoses the **symptom** of a problem and attempts to fix it themselves, without the insight of their followers. More times than not this approach does not provide long-term solutions, and is a telltale sign of an underdeveloped leader with a poor connection to their followers. The outcome is a followers' response that is artificial, and only the minimum effort required to complete any task will be offered. This is a sign of a weak-working relationship.

- The second level of follower response occurs when the leader accurately diagnoses the **source** of a problem, devises a plan of action and then directs their followers to execute the plan. This approach is the mark of a mature leader and lends itself to acquiring sound solutions. The followers' response is good largely due to the leader's ability to effectively communicate the followers' role in the action plan. The follower is committed to completing their part of the process competently, though they are typically unconcerned about how their roles interconnect in totality. This is how most workplace tasks are executed and is indicative of a strong-working relationship.

- The third level occurs when the leader uses a collaborative response of leader/follower to attack the **source** of a problem. The strategy and execution of the plan is done in such a way that the leader demonstrates an intimate knowledge of how their followers think, feel and operate. This approach will reveal that the leader is connected to the **spirit** of the follower. This connection has the potential to yield the greatest level of effort from the follower because of their commitment to the leader, not just the task. With this kind of relationship followers are far more likely to avail their discretionary effort to the leader often without prompt. This is the sign of the consummate working relationship; capable of repeatedly outperforming the efforts of teams that have weak, or even strong working relationships.

According to author Liz Wiseman, using the third approach can grant leaders access to discretionary effort from followers that can produce in the 120th percentile, while other approaches yield less than fifty percent from their followers.[13] Discretionary effort can make a world of difference for a leader, but it isn't given randomly, and accessing it isn't a simple process. One of the most effective methods for gaining access to discretionary effort is to start by building strong working relationships between leader and follower.

LEADERSHIP AND RELATIONSHIPS

The American lifestyle is molded out of convenience. Everything we do has to be scheduled. We've become slaves to our schedules to such a degree that our calendars are our over-lords to which we submit our requests to eat, meet, sleep, work or play. Relationships are anything but convenient, and can never be 'scheduled'. If YOU desire to grow as a leader, and tap the secret reserves of your followers' discretionary effort, YOU must re-model *"YOUR"* attitude. Your time...your family's time...your schedule... your culture...your norms...and your values.... All these YOURS must become OURS—YOU and the follower.

Leadership as a whole is a concept based on theory; however, there are a few facts about leadership that YOU need to be aware of. One such fact is that leadership will expose every personal idiosyncrasy and pet peeve YOU have, despite your greatest efforts to conceal them. For example, if individuals who are unwilling to admit fault easily perturbs YOU, rest assured that peeve will be brought to light. Transparency and light-hearted dialogue on the part of the leader regarding their pet peeves is usually the best deodorant for safeguarding against any miscommunications that could possibly lead to tension between leader and follower. (NOTE: The leader should be willing to hear the pet peeves of followers as well.) The cruel irony about having pet peeves is it seems that YOU can easily identify them in the people you've been charged with leading...real or assumed.

A second fact about leadership is followers consciously monitor how the leader treasures people. Their constant surveillance of the leader takes place on a day-to-day basis, especially during times of adversity and triumph. And its not just people who work directly for the leader, but anyone in the organization is an observer. The Greek philosopher Aristotle believed that the highest form of human activity was *contemplation*. With regard to leadership, I argue that the highest form of leader activity is *communication*.

CASE IN POINT:

Have you ever observed this scene at work? A leader, manager or supervisor is talking on the phone when YOU approach them. When they become aware of your presence they try to conclude their conversation on the phone to meet with YOU, but the person on the other line doesn't recognize their cues. That's when YOU see the leader recklessly make inappropriate facial gestures signifying frustration, accompanied by the rolling motion of their hand, indicating hurry up. Upon the conclusion of the telephone conversation the leader may even apologize for making YOU wait, while offering an excuse for their actions, but they are unaware of the damage that has been done. Although their ambition to assist your needs is admirable, they've inadvertently left YOU feeling devalued – wondering first, who was the person on the other line, and secondly, have they ever done that to me? The actions of the leader in this instance will be sketched in the mind of the follower, and it will take some considerable time and effort to remove it.

In the face of deadlines to meet goals, strained budgets, and a whole host of other underlying leadership dynamics, leaders must remain cognizant about how they treasure ALL people. People are, and will always be, a leader's most precious resource— another fact about leadership.

LEADERSHIP STYLES: "COMMON ENEMY" OR "COMMON GOAL" "COMMON ENEMY"

Remember, the Inevitable Variable states that every industry, project or endeavor will have the constant variables of people and problems (Chapter 3). The natural disputes that occur between people during the realization of a goal should be expected. If these differences are left unchecked however, people's focus on the goal will begin to wane and their bickering can become a major drain on the most precious commodity on the planet—human capital.

The loss of human capital has a cancerous effect on performance and can lead to complete failure. Some leaders know this all too well and deliberately seek to establish a climate that produces an environment in which they, the leader, become the focus of the people's moans and groans. The leader employs a tyrannical approach to management where he or she may be greatly respected, but is equally despised. The followers have an utter disdain for the leader's managerial style, and fear the wrath of the leader to such a degree they hold each other to a very high level of accountability. They even demand perfection from one another, but their commitment to the leader is virtually nonexistent. Though unpopular with subordinates, this style of task-oriented leadership can be brutally effective despite its potentially devastating affect on building viable, long-term working relationships. This approach to leadership is very similar to Douglas McGregor's "Theory X" style of leadership, which assumes that:

- People do not like to work and will avoid work whenever possible;
- People must be forced to work; and
- People are inherently unambitious and irresponsible, seek security and expect to be directed in their work.[14]

"COMMON GOAL"

A style of leadership that is based on a common goal employs a much different course of action than one based on a common enemy. Common goal leaders create a workplace environment that is family oriented and based on relationships, not tasks. They establish a common goal that is palatable, and communicate the vision of that goal in such a way that is maternal in nature, as if they are birthing something—invoking a protective instinct of the goal from the followers. This ensures that the vision is shared and equally valued. Further communication of the vision will provide clear road maps and signposts that illustrate the all-important process, and the followers are shown exactly where they're needed in the process—not to the exclusion of the process, but an integral part of it.

Additionally, leaders who adopt a common goal strategy of leadership establish enthusiasm as the bloodline for workplace motivation. They understand the infectious nature that enthusiasm can have on people and its direct correlation to production, so they're constantly planting seeds of enthusiasm throughout the process. Followers are consistently encouraged to remain passionate during the process, but are cautioned that enthusiasm must never be allowed to override skillset. Managers should manage enthusiastically, supervisors should supervise enthusiastically and workers should work enthusiastically, but everyone should stay in their lanes so the efforts of the collective group are being maximized. When creating an atmosphere of obtaining a common goal, always think of "common" as "communal"—a shared responsibility by everyone in the group to meet the goal.

If there is a *common enemy* that these great leaders create, it is making distractions an adversary. As a leader, once YOU survive some of the customary impediments of leadership such as tradition, an unwillingness of people to adapt, budgetary restrictions, cultural clashes and technological hindrances, for the rest of your tenure as a leader YOU will be overwhelmed with being a *witness*—witness to the lives of the people you lead... their struggles...their losses...their triumphs...their shortcomings... their family arguments...their near break ups... their marriages...

divorces and reconciliations...their complaints of their child's terrible twos...their gripes about their sassy teenagers...their accusations of their grown children's inability to take the time to call and check on them...their regretful expressions of being a lousy mother or father...their burden of placing a parent in a senior citizen home...their dissatisfaction with the state of the world...and their failing physical health. And most of all, YOU witness their emotional instability, which has a direct correlation on their ability to focus and produce at work.

Your job as a leader is to somehow consider the weightier matters of their heart, while simultaneously nudging followers progressively toward the realization of the corporate goal. It is incumbent upon the leader to constantly recreate models of motivation in the minds of the followers that spotlight the process, and redirect their focus back to the manifestation of the goal. Here's the hard truth: anything that distracts the focus of the follower is an enemy of the process. And nothing, including the followers themselves, can be allowed to jeopardize the process, and ultimately the manifestation of the goal.

Lastly, great leaders establish a covenant with their followers, and forecast the likelihood of these distractions. They set parameters on how the team will manage distractions. These parameters have a dual purpose: First, parameters are designed to protect the relationship between leaders and followers. Familiarity breeds contempt. A pronounced reverence and respect for the office of the leader should be afforded by the follower, despite the naturally occurring human tendency to become 'chummy' during repeated human interactions. Second, setting parameters shield the manifestation of the goal from unlikely delays, which could be caused by any of the previously mentioned distractions. A clear demarcation of these parameters and full comprehension of them will serve as:

- Natural guidelines for strong leader-follower working relationships.
- Appropriate workplace dialogue.
- Acceptable peer group behavior that positively affects production.

Appropriate workplace dialogue and acceptable peer group behavior are two vital elements when leading people to meet a corporate goal and should remain at the forefront of the leader's mind.

DYNAMO PAK: "USING LEADERSHIP GAMBITS TO MAXIMIZE PERFORMANCE"

Author Robert Cialdini offers a very practical illustration regarding a complex experiment conducted about reciprocity. In summation, a university professor sent Christmas cards to a sample of strangers. There were an overwhelming number of people who sent cards in return, with the vast majority of those never inquiring about the sender. Though small in scope, the study discovered the rule of reciprocity—that, "We should try to repay, in kind, what another person has provided for us."[15] This obligation, for lack of a better term, has been the subject of much debate in leadership and business conferences that broach the topic of how leaders should ethically drive the efforts of followers. What's the difference between motivation and manipulation; tactics or trickery; coercion or compulsion? Money bonuses and fear of termination are still the two most common workplace drivers; despite decades of empirical data that suggests neither build strong working relationships.[16] So what are some ethical ways leaders can progress people toward the realization of a corporate goal, while demonstrating an endearing appreciation for followers that will ultimately lead to the rule of reciprocity and access their discretionary effort? One such way is with the use of Gambits.

Gambits are strategically planned maneuvers where a present day sacrifice will compel a feeling of repayment in the future. Unlike the carrot at the end of the stick where we coerce our children into getting good grades while dangling a gift out in front of them, with gambits the leader incurs the debt of a transgression by a follower, and then leverages the pardon for greater support in the future.

For example, an employee oversleeps and is late to work. YOU, the leader, could document the tardy arrival, or give them a break based on the reality that at some point doing the year someone else is going to oversleep and be late to work. If the tardy employee is mature, YOU can expect that he or she, as well as their co-workers, will appreciate being absolved. And based on the rule of reciprocity, feel a need to return the favor to YOU by putting forth more effort towards arriving to work on time in the future. The gambit here is that the leader will absorb the penalty of the tardy arrival in expectation that all employees will value the reprieve granted and recommit to on time arrivals for not just work, but meetings as well. The whole idea of the gambit is to leverage a minor hiccup, against the possibility of a major jump in progression toward a corporate goal.

There is a thin line between gambits and coercion so it is imperative that leaders who use gambits are ethically and morally sound. Gambits are a bit of a gamble and could very easily backfire, but the reward could outweigh the risk. If exercised correctly, leadership gambits are very effective in gaining access to an employee's discretionary effort.

Another kind of leadership gambit is called an "empathy expense." An empathy expense does not cost the leader personally and there are no charges levied against the company, but it can be as good as gold. There's no denying that providing industrial resources is paramount to leading people. People need the right tools to do the job. And when a follower has a real need such as a health issue or a family commitment, it's only prudent for a leader to put to use any company benefits to reconcile that need. But when a follower has just a mere desire (not a real need), the leader can use a gambit to appease the follower. Some of the best opportunities for bolstering strong workplace relationships and tapping into an employees' discretionary effort can occur when the leader utilizes an empathy expense.

Example: A follower shares with a leader that they've made a pact with several friends to lose weight, citing that they're bothered by the fact that they can't be as active with their kids as they'd like to be. The follower has found a great rate with a very reputable trainer. The meeting times for this fitness boot camp are 9:00 a.m. and again at 2:00 p.m. But company policy limits what the leader can do to help the follower. So what are some options?

Rescheduling work hours may accommodate one of the meeting times, but the chief reason for the success of the boot camp is the intense, hard-hitting approach of two-a-days for the first six weeks of the program.

How about this? The leader could meet with the other followers in the department individually and create a personal and professional development 'wish list' by asking the followers what are some of their wants and desires for work and home. What the leader will discover is that every follower has both needs and wants, though some will never voice either without this platform.

The leader can then create a P&PD (personal and professional development) calendar and visibly post it within the work section. Once the leader has met with everyone and completed the wish list, they'll quickly discover that Stephanie's desire to be off three consecutive Thursdays in March to work at the shelter to raise animal cruelty awareness can be leveraged against Charles's desire to be off by 2:30 p.m. for the month of September so that he can attend his son's select soccer practices. In April, YOU (the leader) volunteered to cover the lunch hour so that the admins could attend the annual art festival, which influences the custodial crew to come in on a Saturday to unlock the facility so that Bryce, Velma and Aaron can make up for lost time at the boot camp. Though YOU tried to keep the P&PD calendar in house, the department on the fourth floor had a couple of special needs during the summer months that could easily be plugged in, and the Research & Development guys, who are good friends with the custodians are willing to do just about anything for a chance to be off for the entire weekend leading up to the Super Bowl in February!

Even if the calendar cannot meet all the wants and desires of the entire section, followers will find it especially gratifying that the leader was willing to be empathetic to their *needs, wants* and *desires*. Empathy expenses are an ethical approach to motivating people and in exchange you'll find out that people are willing to offer ten, fifteen or twenty-five percent extra discretionary effort that other leaders may not have received otherwise.

Yet another leadership gambit is education. The Inevitable Variable states that when it comes to communication, there will always be people and problems. But when it comes to leadership, the Inevitable Variables are a shortage of money and qualified personnel. So with no money and limited resources, what leadership gambits can YOU use? Education. An unknown author said, *"Sometimes training is nothing more than skills and competencies for now. Education, on the other hand, provides skills and competencies for the future."* Educational opportunities are typically less expensive than training events. Giving people a sense of marketability boosts morale and is an excellent method of professional development that is mutually beneficial for the company and employee. As YOU learn more about the people YOU lead, become familiar with their career aspirations so that YOU can be proactive in seeking educational opportunities for them. The P&PD calendar can help. To remain fair and ethical, exercise a strong working knowledge of **Dog Loyalty** and **Cat Loyalty**.

Dog loyalty is devotion to the person (employee). Cat loyalty is devotion to the house (company). As a leader, YOU have to balance the needs and wants of the follower with the requirements and expectations of the administration. Remember our tardy employee? YOU accepted the late arrival of the employee in hopes that it wouldn't become a pattern, and would instead translate to consistent on time arrivals. This is an example of Dog Loyalty. However, if the employees' late arrivals became habitual, then company policy would dictate administrative actions—Cat Loyalty.

Note: Because YOU treasure people, YOU may feel that leaders should only utilize dog loyalty. YOU could probably recall the cat loyal supervisors you've experienced who were strictly by the book, who offered followers little wiggle room, or who despised working in the gray area. But cat loyalty does offer some guidelines that actually help to protect the dog loyalty element between leader and follower. YOU need to use both. Depending on the company and culture of the people YOU lead, a safe starting point is a 55/45 ratio of dog loyalty/cat loyalty. My experience has been, the closer YOU get to employing an 80/20 combination of dog/cat loyalty, the more a followers' discretionary effort will be granted to YOU, and the higher their output.

The last leadership gambit I'd like to list is one involving disciplinary action. An extremely critical opportunity to connect with an employee and cultivate a strong working relationship, as well as an opportunity to access their discretionary effort actually involves the discipline process. But first allow me to argue what should be the two primary functions of discipline:

- Penalize undesirable behavior
- Correct or modify future behavior in the form of professional development.

There is a grave error that I see supervisors, managers, and leaders routinely make regarding discipline—they do not fully adhere to the second function of discipline, which is to use professional development to modify future behavior. Instead, they extend the penalty phase of the first function by reassigning the employee to a less desirable position, or some other version of the proverbial "dog house" after punishment has been administered. Upon completion of the discipline phase, if the employee is remorseful and exhibits a desire to reform, the leader needs to quickly reengage the employee through the use of professional development, not professional distancing.

Professional distancing happens when a leader views a subordinate as a problem child, and begins to systematically document their screw-ups. Documentation is fine; but it's their motivation behind the documentation that is in question. I sometimes find that their reasons for documenting the followers' infractions isn't to design remedies for corrective action prior to a gross violation, but to distance themselves as far away from the scene of the crime when the follower finally crashes and burns.

Instead, take the opportunity to professionally develop the individual by *bridging* a connection to them, not distancing yourself away from them. Map out some 'low hanging fruit goals,' which can be easily accomplished to boost their confidence. Restoring their confidence is extremely vital, and cannot be overstated.

Secondly, complete a strengths inventory. The use of Gallup polls, years of research data and thousands of interviews say, "In the workplace, when an organizations' leadership fails to focus on an individual's strengths, the odds of an employee being engaged are a dismal 1 in 11 (9%). But when the organizations' leadership focuses on the strengths of its employees, the odds soar to almost 3 in 4 (73%)."[17]

People's minds are often cluttered during the discipline process so they naturally gravitate toward something they can focus on. Make that focus YOU. The gambit here is your "adoption" of them at an emotionally sensitive point in their career, which could translate to a rejuvenated effort on their part. When people recognize the presence of your support, they will feel indebted to YOU. Now redirect their aim toward restoring their professional reputation, and use their newfound discretionary energy and effort toward meeting the company's goals while they are re-engaged back into the workplace environment.

CHAPTER 7

HOW TO MANAGE YOU FOR SUCCESS

R.E.C.O.I.L. Management

YOU purchased this book because of the challenge to be successful. The stress of that challenge has left *you* seeking for ways to empower YOU. Your search for excellence may have frustrated YOU along the way, but YOU kept trying and YOU refused to give up. My hope now is that YOU have yet another tool to meet the many challenges to be successful. So I gladly say to YOU...light your fuse top performer, YOU are Sittin' on Dyno-Might!

YOU now posses the power to achieve great things when YOU unveil your Dyno-Might! People will marvel at this new, enhanced YOU and ask: What is Dyno-Might?

Dyno-Might is:

- Your willingness to be authentic.
- Your capacity to overcome.
- Your emotional intelligence.
- Your ideas that bring about change.
- Your ECHO that rings loud.
- Your commitment to relationships that compels people to give YOU 120% of their effort.

Each stick of Dyno-Might alone can elevate YOU to greater and greater heights, but when YOU put them all together, KA BOOM! How do YOU manage all of this newfound power to maximize your abilities? YOU manage your Dyno-Might! with the use of *R.E.C.O.I.L. Management.*

R.E.C.O.I.L. Management is a decision-making model, a business operating system and professional development tool all in one. With *R.E.C.O.I.L. Management* the decisions YOU make **Reflect Ethics,** your ideas and solutions **Communicate Outlook** and YOU use **Influence** to **Lead** people—all of which will take your career to the next level. Your dialogue and decisive actions will champion your career path.

YOU will face many obstacles during your career, and YOU will triumph over them. There may even be attacks on your personal integrity, but YOU will prevail. And there will be instances when YOU will be denied time and time again, but YOU will eventually win. YOU will win because YOU never stopped aiming at the target. The treacherous seas of a career path can sometimes obscure your aim, but ***R.E.C.O.I.L. Management*** keeps your aim on target. What's the target YOU ask? Here's the answer, and the culminating point of this book: Harmony.

HARMONY

The target isn't a dream position, or a big promotion or even retirement for that matter. The target is **Harmony**: a constant state of awareness that joins YOU with your surroundings; that keeps YOU connected to people; that builds strong relationships; that ensures YOU remain relevant; that makes YOU compatible; that encourages YOU to continue to learn, that allows YOU to blend in and then stand out, all while simultaneously co-existing in **Harmony** with other "YOUs".

Now go make music on the great stage of life, top performer. Your audience awaits YOU. Take aim...light your fuse...and go blow 'em away!

ENDNOTES

1. *90 Minute Workout: Leadership Training Manual* by Dr. Charles Moody Jr. Copyright 2013 Austin, TX.
2. Advertising Age Magazine, June, 25 2012. http://adage.com/article/datacenter-advertising-spending/100-leading-national-advertisers/234882/
3. Immanuel Kant's and the Categorical Imperative, by Shandon L. Guthrie. (Published in *The Examined Life On-Line Philosophy Journal*, Volume II Issue 7).
4. Journal of Occupational & Organizational Psychology Dec.2007 by Byron Kristen. http://onlinelibrary.wiley.com/doi/10.1111/joop.2007.80.issue-4/issuetoc
5. *The Inner Game of Tennis, The Classic Guide to the Mental Side of Peak Perfection* by Timothy Galway, Random House, 2008. P
6. *The Purple Cow* by Seth Godin. Penguin Group, 2002. P
7. *Getting Past No Negotiation in Difficult Situations* by William Ury. Bantam 1993 *p*
8. *Communication Excellence, Change Your Words, Change Your World* by Brian Polansky, Arrow Ridge Publishing, 2005.
9. The Sword of No Sword: Life of the Master Warrior Tesshu by John Stevens, Shambalam 2001.

10. *The Geographical Analysis of Population, 1994. http://www.genetics.org/content/140/2/767.short*

11. *Intelligence Led Policing,* by Jerry Ratcliffe. Wilan Publishing Devon, UK 2008.

12. *Teaching to Save Lives: Seven Proven Ways to Make Your Teaching Come Alive* by Howard Hendricks, Multnomah Books, 1987.

13. *Multipliers: How the Best Leaders Make Everyone Smarter by Liz Wiseman* Harper Collins, 2010.

14. *The Human Side to Enterprise,* by Douglas McGregor, McGraw Hill 2006.

15. *Influence: Science and Practice,* by Robert Cialdini, Harper Business, 2006.

16. *Hertzberg on Motivation,* by Frederick Herzberg, Industry Week, 1991.

17. *Strengths Based Leadership: Great Team, Leaders and Why People Follow* by Tom Rath and Barry Conchie, Gallup Press, NY, 2009.

BIBLIOGRAPHY

Aamodt, Michael G. and Bobbie Raynes. *Human Relations in Business*. Wadsworth (Paperback), Boston, MA 2000.

Bassham, Lanny. *With Winning in Mind*, 2nd edition, World/ Olympic Champion, 1995.

Baron, Robert A., Robert Byrne. *Social Psychology*, 12th edition. Allyn and Bacon, While Plains, NY, 2008.

Brown, Duane. *Career Counseling and Career Development*, 9th edition.
Allyn and Bacon, While Plains, NY, 2006

Carson, Dana. *Incarnational Leadership: Leading From Their Shoes*. Dana
Carson Ministries, 2011.

Cialdini, Robert. *Influence: Science and Practice*, 5th edition, Harper Business, 2006.

Cordner, Gary W. *Police Administration*, 7th edition. Anderson Publishing,
Cincinnati, OH, 2010.

Drucker, Peter F. *Management Challenges for the 21st Century*, Harper Business, 2001.

Enos, Brian, Kris Knuckler. *Practical Shooting: Beyond Fundamentals*, Zediker, 1990.

Fletcher, Connie. *What Cops Know*. Pocket Books, NY, 1990.

Gallway, Timothy. *The Inner Game of Tennis, The Classic Guide to the Mental Side of Peak Perfection*. Random House 2008 (originally published 1974).

Godin, Seth. *The Purple Cow*, Penguin Group, 2002.

Greene, Robert. *The 48 Laws of Power*, Penguin Books, 2001.

Handy, Charles. *The Age of Paradox*. Harvard Business Review,1995.

Heller, Robert, Tim Hindle. *Essential Manager's Manual*, DK Publishing, 1998.

Hendricks, Howard. *Teaching to Save Lives: Seven Proven Ways to Make Your Teaching Come Alive*. Multnomah Books, 1987.
Hertzberg, Frederick. *Hertzberg on Motivation,* Industry Week, 1991.

McGregor, Douglas. *The Human Side of Enterprise.* McGraw Hill, 2006.

Meese, Edwing III and P. J. Ortmeier. *Leadership, Ethics and Policing.* 2nd edition, Prentice Hall, 2009.

Miltenberger, Raymond. *Behavior Modification.* Wadsworth, Cengage Learning, Belmont, CA, 2008.

Neal, James E. Jr. Effective Phrases for Performance Appraisals, 1978
Polansky, Brian. *Communication Excellence: Change Your Words, Change Your World.* Arrow Ridge Publishing, 2005.

Ratcliffe, Jerry. *Intelligence Led Policing*, Wilan Publishing Devon, UK 2008.

Rath, Tom and Barry Conchie, *Strengths Based Leadership: Great Team, Leaders and Why People Follow.* Gallup Press, NY, 2009.

Schultz, Duane and Sydney Ellen Schultz. *Psychology & Work Today*, 8th edition. Prentice Hall 1998.

Senge, Peter M. *The Fifth Discipline: the Art and Practice of the Learning Organization.*   Random House, 1990.

Stevens, John. The Sword of No Sword: Life of the Master Warrior Tesshu, Shambalam 2001.

Thaler, Richard H. and Cass R. Sustein. *Nudge: Improving Decisions about Health, Wealth and Happiness*, Penguin Group, 2008.

Wiseman, Liz and Greg McKeown. *Multipliers: How the Best Leaders Make Everyone Smarter*. Harper Collins, 2010.

Ury, William. *Getting Past No: Negotiation in Difficult Situations*. Bantam 1993.

ABOUT THE AUTHOR

Antoine Lane is a dynamic speaker and exceptional trainer. His unique ability to maximize human energy and effort is his trademark. He holds a Masters degree in Training and Professional Development, with heavy academic emphasis in Human Performance Technology. Additionally, Antoine is a Certified Public Manager (CPM) allowing him to consult in both private and public sector entities. He's the Executive Director of Training Lanes—a professional development company that offers services in corporate training and professional firearms training. To learn more about Antoine Lane, please visit his website at www.traininglanes.com.